Alain de Vulpian

Irène Dupoux-Couturier

Preface by Peter Senge

Translation by Richard Maxwell

HOMO SAPIENS
Collapse or Fulfillment

The humanist metamorphosis

Happymorphose
9 Rue Portalis
75008 Paris

www.happymorphose.com

HAPPYMORPHOSE

© Happymorphose, 2022

Graphic design : Sophie Juin

Layout work : Claire-Agnès Gueutin

All Rights Reserved

Impression : BoD - Book on Demand

Norderstedt, Deutschland

ISBN: 978-2-9568559-4-1

Dépôt légal : mars 2022

> *Our history today is of man's growing awareness...*
> *Everywhere we see interactions at work*
> *making our universe so coherent, so beautiful, so mysterious.*

Ilya Prigogine, Interview Libre Belgique,
21 november 2002

> *The biological-technical-digital metamorphosis needs above all to be accompanied, regulated, controlled, guided by an ethical-cultural-social metamorphosis.*

Edgar Morin, Knowledge, Ignorance, Mystery

> *At the pinnacle of life, fulfillment*

Antonio Damasio, The Strange Order of Things: Life, Feeling, and the Making of Cultures

> *In living systems everything is in motion; even stable situations result from movements which by combining maintain an equilibrium.*

Alain de Vulpian, Éloge de la métamorphose,
en marche vers une nouvelle humanité

Summary

Preface 9
Foreword.. 21
Introduction 25

PART I
HOMO SAPIENS 27

Chapter 1. Living systems 29
From divine plan to the darwinian revolution 30
The prism of living.. 31
Living systems are subject to bifurcations 34
Bifurcation today: uncertainties and
return to being human 37

Chapter 2. Understanding the metamorphoses
of Homo Sapiens 41
Homo sapiens is a socio-cultural animal 41
Homo sapiens is a social animal that lives in networks ... 46

PART II
THE SOCIO-CULTURAL METAMORPHOSES
OF HOMO SAPIENS... 51

Chapter 3. From hunter-gatherers to
the age of civilizations 53

Chapter 4. European metamorphoses 57
First metamorphosis: the renaissance
and the era of rationality 58
Second metamorphosis: 20th-21st centuries,
flourishing personalism 59
The change in personalities: four major transformations 64
A new living social fabric 71
Society-as-a-brain 78

Chapter 5. The rise of spirituality 81
Homo sapiens, spiritual animal 81
Societal debate includes the unconscious 91
Learning to dialogue with one's brain: take breaks 92
Myths of the future 93
A century of the mind and of the spirit 97

PART III
A GREAT BIFURCATION:
HESITATIONS IN HUMANIST METAMORPHOSIS 103

Chapter 6. Towards a living societal economy 105
The new creatures: hybrid collectivities 106
Metamorphosis feeds on itself 114
A new economy of sharing and cooperation 116

Chapter 7. From a hyper-financial capitalism to the new socio-economy 119
1970s and 1980s: companies seek to support the evolution of people 119
1990s: the financialization of capitalism hinders the metamorphosis of large companies 122
2010-2020: some large companies are opening to metamorphosis 124

Chapter 8. The digital revolution: from the portable computer to "Artificial Intelligence" 131
The web and portable phones are transforming the world 131
Information technologies are a source of life 133
Society-as-ant-hill: a frightening future 136
Society-as-a-brain: artificial intelligence as an opportunity 139
AI and education 142
Metamorphosis and artificial intelligence are complementary 145

Chapter 9. Towards a participative democracy 153
Representative democracy reaches a dead end 153
Societal coagulations, collective emotions and the anger of the people 160
Paths for the future: what lessons can we learn? 166

Possible evolution towards a participative societal democracy: the role of collective intelligence 171

Chapter 10. Towards a planet-wide metamorphosis: East and West 173
The challenges are planet-wide 175
The euro-american civilization has rubbed off on the world 177
Western and chinese civilizations 179
American and european uncertainties 184

Chapter 11. And what about Europe? 191
Another Europe is putting itself together 192
Europeans-as-a-brain.. 198
Is a european "soft power" scenario feasible? 200

Chapter 12. Conclusion. Intuiting a change of era: we must take care of our humanist metamorphosis 205
The intuition of a changing era 207
Taking care of metamorphosis 208

Bibliography 211
Acknowledgements 217

Preface

All species survive in a niche. Indeed, one view of evolution is that the niche and the species co-evolve - each allowing the other to be both viable and resilient. In this era of anxiety about the future, it is useful to know that there are many examples of human societies flourishing for tens of thousands of years. But, these exemplars of social-ecological harmony are all local (Indians in America or aboriginal people in Australia). Today, we are living a different question, "Can such harmony be realized by humans living in the 'niche' of planet Earth?" What would this require in terms of beliefs, assumptions, behaviors and sensibilities?

The French anthropo-sociologist Alain de Vulpian has been studying the transformations of Western society for 60 years. Inspired by Carl Rogers, he has been using an in-depth investigation method in the field to collect "weak signals". I first discovered Alain's work at the SoL[1] Global Forum in Vienna in 2005 where he shared with us his view of learning organization taking part in the 'process of civilization'.[2] Following Francisco Varela and Humberto Maturana, de Vulpian looks at the world through the prism of Living and sees humans today at a bifurcation point with very different possible futures ahead of us. "We are not living through a crisis but rather a metamorphosis of society", he says preferring this Greek biological term to the more mechanical Latin word, transformation, feeling that it illuminates subtle ways open to influencing what might unfold.

---
1. Society for Organization Learning
2. Norbert Elias, *Uber den prozess der Zivilisation*, 1939.

As an anthropologist, he sees Homo Sapiens as a socio-cultural animal capable of adapting to various environments. This is our great strength and our liability, for adaptation can be mal-adaptation and does not assure enhancement of well-being. He points out that the socio-cultural evolution of Homo Sapiens seems to be much faster than in most other species, in part because of the extreme plasticity of the human brain. He describes the various rapid metamorphoses from the hunter harvesters to the age of modern civilization over the past 40,000 years and argues that today's digital revolution needs to be seen in the context of Homo Sapiens' place on the planet and our capacity to enhance or erode the well-being of many species as well as our own.

In particular, de Vulpian's analysis of the process of civilization since the beginning of the 20th century has led him to the hypothesis that we are on the cusp of "a new era for humanity", the impact of which could be as significant as the transition from the feudal era to the Renaissance. This new humanism would supplant the myths of progress, competition, maximization and success with the pursuit of individual well-being through cooperation and optimization of larger systems. "Hunter gatherers made more use of the emotional-relational and spiritual dimensions of their brain" because their living was so intertwined with those of other species and their living systems, upon whom they depended. "But by the 17th century, Europeans began to accentuate the rational dimension", which has driven both Western science and more recently the Western economic model, based on growth in production and consumption.

"Perhaps for the first time on a large scale, humans in the 21st century could now simultaneously engage the four dimensions of the brain: spiritual, emotional-relational, sensorial and rational."

This hypothesis builds from de Vulpian's view that the past centuries, first in the West and now spreading, have witnessed an arc of increasing individualism – "ordinary people" drawn into a society of consumers have felt themselves become individual persons but individuals embedded within a larger materialistic economic reality rather than a living reality. The result has been separation from one another and from other life, which many people are starting to see as a by-product of our material progress.

People are beginning to become aware that our immense scientific and technical progress, the fruit of human rationality pushed to the extreme, could give rise to ecological and geopolitical catastrophes threatening the very survival of the human species.

De Vulpian believes this growth in awareness is giving rise to the beginnings of an "ecological consciousness," a key axis of our current metamorphosis. "The sociocultural and neurobiological revolution of the human brain at the end of the 20th century is fostering a new "globally connected, enmeshed and entangled world, a world which leaves an important place for local projects and initiatives but which enables their results to be shared around the planet". De Vulpian calls this new world "a brain-like-society - it is heterarchical with its members being on an equal footing. It is a society of individual persons, of startups, of social businesses, of young interconnected entrepreneurs, of smart networks that bring together regional state authorities, non-profit organizations, local businesses and smart cities". De Vulpian calls these "collective hybrids", "new living creatures" who are restructuring the world. Evoking Pierre Teilhard de Chardin, he describes this collective consciousness as a global thin film of thought, a "we-sphere".

While his focus on weak signals has led De Vulpian to see a new, self-organizing ecologically attuned society as an evolutionary possibility, the bifurcation of metamorphosis can easily tip in a very different direction. "The entrenched powers (nation states, politicians, large traditional businesses and institutions) are blocking the metamorphosis".

We do not need to look hard for evidence of this, as around the world we see the rise of populism and violence and a surge of strong autocratic leaders. In a previous book in 2015, de Vulpian wrote, "Our people are suffering and are demoralized. They accuse the governmental elites of being responsible for their misfortune and are contesting them brutally in the polls and in the street. Serious political crises could disrupt the metamorphosis". Driven by anger at the failures of "representative democracy" and through fear of continuing economic dislocation, many ordinary people are voting for strong leaders even if these leaders actually violate their own espoused values and embody a much more totalitarian and controlling world view. In desperation, we are reverting to the old-time style of leadership. As often is the case, deep change rarely proceeds in a linear fashion. The very disruptions signaling new possibilities also create threat, and when the threat and fear dominate, other parts of our brain take over, we become 'emotionally high-jacked' and, as neuroscientists say, "the brain downshifts to its more primitive fight-flight-freeze options".

Contemporary media, both mass media and the newer social media, continually reinforce the focus on these immediate surface changes. But "the political and economic dynamics are but a small part of the problem. The deep core issues are neither social nor economic. They are cultural. Humans are not in control." We are part of the web of life. But most of us live with very little connection to this larger web. We act as if we are separate from nature. As de Vulpian shows, this problem is not only linked to the Industrial era, but has its roots in the Neolithic era, when many societies shaped by organized agriculture, private land ownership and the accumulation of personal wealth started to live by this erroneous notion of separation.

The myth of separation leaves us blind to seeing the most challenging issues of the day, from climate change to massive South-North human migrations (many of which are 'climate refugees'), are actually products of our own making. Seeing them as disconnected from our ways of living, we react as if we had nothing to do with their origins. Ironically, this is an old story. Human beings have a long history of altering their natural environment and denying the social and ecological consequences. Many local cultures, even quite sophisticated ones, over-expanded, exceeding their water supply or destroying their topsoil or habitat. Today's situation is no different. It is just unfolding on a new scale.

De Vulpian's book offers more than just an alert. It aims to help ordinary people be more or less *clairvoyant*, to strengthen their intuitions and to innovate. At the bifurcation point, by paying attention to the weak signals we can "take care of metamorphosis". From this perspective, for example, "Climate change is a great gift if we accept it". We have to change our way of living to be in harmony with the larger natural systems.

The problem, of course, is that such cultural evolution takes time, while the accumulating environmental and social disruptions playing out around us are creating a great sense of urgency. Alternatively, de Vulpian believes learning to pay attention to the weak signals leads to seeing the cultural evolution that is already unfolding all around us.

Consider the global movement toward basic new ways of thinking about education. Few institutions more embody the norms of a culture than the way we educate our children. While radical change may be most visible in higher education (e.g., MOOCs, massively open online courses, and other means of distributing education beyond the control of universities), what MIT's president Rafael Raif calls the "democratization of education" is just as evident, and even more important, in the "upstream" institutions of primary and secondary education.

Children do not need schools in order to learn. Before they ever enter school, young children are learning continually, understanding the complex physical, social and emotional systems of growing and living. Facing issues, children accept paradox and ambiguity. They know how to learn from nature to survive. Noticing these simple facts can alert us to another cornerstone of humans living in great harmony with nature. There is a saying in ancient Chinese culture that "the mark of every Golden age is that children are the most important members of society and teaching the most revered profession". The beneficiaries are not just the children but us all. Our connection with children connects us to the essence of learning - curiosity, openness and play – which are also vital for innovation in any work setting. They fill our lives with joy and mystery. And, we forge an emotional connection with the future. Through the eyes of the child, the future is no longer an abstraction, a loose bundle of concepts and projections, but a living reality. When we lose this connection, it becomes much easier to "discount the future", as economists say. The result is one of our deepest cultural problems, our short-positions are often more masculine than the men they succeed because they are forced to prove themselves in the terms of masculine models. Still, we have been watching the practical consequences of this shift unfold for many years: almost twenty years ago within the SoL Sustainability Consortium. Many of our best examples of corporations making genuine progress in integrating social and ecological well-being into their strategy had women in key leadership roles. Why? Because they were masterful at building the larger networks of collaboration needed to realize such changes. Focusing on relationships, building networks, and creating space for change to develop rather than "driving change". These are the new skills for leading systemic change and they are classic feminine ways of leading.

As we learn how to pay attention to such weak signals amidst confusion and emotional cross-currents, we cultivate what de Vulpian calls "socio-perception", a mixture of intuition and empathy to better understand subtle changes in our environment, whereby we "collect weak signals to create scenarios for the future, the roots for shared visions as images of the future at work today".

De Vulpian believes that "because of the process of metamorphosis that has been going on for a century, more and more ordinary people are becoming socio-perceptive, able to feel the interactions between people, networks and society, developing the potential to be more far-seeing". Yet two great counterforces are also at work, both linked to the growing influence of media over this same time period. The first has to do with emotions, the second with information.

Paradoxically, one key to developing socio-perception, especially in today's world, lies in cultivating a level of sightedness and inability to balance the short- and term.

Understanding this, even if dimly, it is no surprise in this age of stress and discontinuity, all around world new educational models are emerging that s the dominant Industrial age paradigm of linear school to include social emotional learning, collaborat learning, project-based learning, systems thinking a design thinking, and what in China are called 'flipp classrooms' where students and teachers learn togetl rather than in the traditional one-way model. 21st centu skills and capacities are gradually receiving their d from government departments as well, more and mo of which are realizing they can either stand on by tl sideline regulating educational programs and watchir schools educate students for jobs that no longer exist, c they can become part of shaping the future. Connecte in many ways to this renaissance, at MIT there is a sayin that schools today need to focus on developing capacities "to do what machines cannot do" – cultivating capacities like imagination, empathy, collaboration, creativity, and caring.

Other key weak signals de Vulpian points to include subtle shifts in language and the rise of women in leadership roles. Examples of the former include shift from "planification" to "search for meaning", from "win-lose competition" to "cooperation and shared vision", from "excellence" to "vitality and resilience", and, using another word from nature, from "maximization" to "blossoming" or "opening up". Regarding leadership, the consequences of the gradual rise of the feminine to counterbalance the hyper-masculinity of our present leadership models, like so many facets of deep change, can be confusing. Ironically, the first generations of women in leadership emotional maturity. "Metamorphosis is characterized by the ability of an organization, a family, a society to self-regulate and to find balance". Perceiving the new requires imaginative as well as sensory awareness. But, fear cramps imagination. Anger polarizes vision. Numbness comes from over-saturation with fear and anger - all of which are epidemic in today's media-driven societies immersed in "news" as entertainment, designed to be emotionally manipulative.

De Vulpian points out that our competing media, while different in their structures and technologies, have become ever more invasive in controlling information. In traditional vertical communication, the mass media, newspapers, editors, and political parties shaped public opinion. In today's more horizontal mode, social media initial appear to be turning things upside down. But such perceptions can be deceptive. The "direct democracy" expressed through freely outspoken public opinion is in fact controlled by a small number of powerful social media corporations, and is not at all the sort of collective intelligence needed.

Today's social media-enabled online "communities" represent a new social engineering dynamic driving socio-perception. But shaped by invisible programmers who create the rules designed to give us what we want to see, and driven by business models aimed at only maximizing attention, they are not self-organized at all, because there is no free or balanced access to information. They are the opposite of real communities which only arise when, in the words of Margaret Wheatley, "you are stuck with each other" - when you have to deal with the fact that someone might actually think and like something that you don't. By contrast, the social media communities of today are extensions of the teenage clique structures, people amassing friends to buffer them against the threats of difference.

We may be waking up to the dangers of manipulated social media, but will we wake up fast enough? A recent article in the New York Times[3] tells how a great many Silicon Valley executives put their children in schools where they have no gadgets because they know how addictive technology can be, particularly for young children, and how unethical it is. Living in the middle of this, they know the way the business world can feed off of fostering addictive behaviors, like junk food businesses who for years have targeted young children with foods heavy with salt and sugar to cultivate these addictions. The retired head of the NSA and CIA, Michael Hayden, with whom SoL worked for several years on fostering greater collaboration within NSA, published a recent book entitled "The Assault on Intelligence: American National Security in an Age of Lies." In it he wonders if such a thing as collective pursuit of the truth isn't impossible in a society where more and more people get their news feeds from social media. Clicks are more important than the truth, wrote the Swedish media expert Ian Scherman.

Taken together, it is a confusing picture. Much is getting better and much is getting worse – which is exactly what de Vulpian means by a bifurcation point. "Homo Sapiens is an extremely inventive, creative animal but he doesn't see the reality, the future, and its dynamics", says de Vulpian. He points out that in this age of profound crosscurrents, none of us can see very far ahead.

So, while the human being has this immense capacity to learn and adapt, the key is to continue to cultivate a sort

---

3. Nellie Bowles, A Dark Consensus about Screens and Kids Begins to Emerge in Silicon Valley, NY Times, Oct 26, 2018.

of neutral *awareness*. While it is easy to be emotionally hijacked by all that makes us fearful or otherwise attracts our attention, it takes real commitment to the future to try as best we can to simply hold it all, something Alain de Vulpian has been practicing for sixty years.

In the end, de Vulpian thinks much will depend on a growing understanding of human spiritual nature, what he calls "a metamorphosis based on the role of emotional and spiritual aspects deeply linked to a new open type of rationality."

While much of his analysis focuses on the West, in my opinion some of the key pivots may be in the East. The Indians and Chinese are latecomers to this delirious party of materialistic economic growth at any cost, watching Western materialism overrun their traditional cultures in the last few decades. This rapid cultural change may prove a paradoxical advantage – subtle, deep losses may prove more discernible when the process unfolds quickly. Time will tell. Much of the growing political assertiveness of the Chinese today, for example, may be rooted in a determination to slow or entirely turn the cultural hegemony of the West. Not many years ago I was in conversation in Beijing with a member of the Central Committee of the Chinese Communist Party, when he observed, "Our pursuit of (material) well-being today may have its roots in a confusion. The ultimate meaning of living is the harmony between human being and nature. To me, there is but one destiny for human being, either to be in harmony with nature, or to be destroyed with the earth".

As these cross-cultural dynamics play out in the coming decades, we will all be well served by keeping Alain de

Vulpian's question in mind: "at the crossroads, awareness is essential to search for new directions".

Peter M. Senge

January 3, 2019

Foreword

In high school after the Second World War, I wondered what could have been done to break the harmful chain of events that led to Stalinist communism, Nazism and tens of millions of deaths. As students at Sciences Po at the end of the 1940s, we wondered about the potential ways of modernity. Democracy and peace were restored, our old exhausted country was going to modernize, but we still had to find the right ways to do it. Some looked to America, others to Russia. Some of my fellow students felt we needed fieldwork to explore how people and society were changing, and what development opportunities these changes were opening or closing.

For more than 60 years, with teams of sociologists and anthropologists from Cofremca, Sociovision and their allies in Europe and North America, I have been observing people, their socio-systems and their organizations in the process of living and changing, trying to understand the dynamics pulling them along; by relying on these areas of research, we have been able to help numerous businesses, administrations and certain political leaders to anticipate the future and to choose paths for development and promising innovations.

It turns out that during the twentieth century, Euro-American socio-culture began a radical transformation, a spontaneous metamorphosis that is continuing into the twenty-first century. I use the word metamorphosis because it evokes an extremely complex biological process[4].

Animals undergo metamorphosis. The caterpillar becomes a butterfly, the tadpole becomes a frog. In the same way civilizations can, like ours, undergo metamorphosis.

Homo Sapiens is a socio-cultural animal. The remarkable plasticity of our central nervous system has enabled us to take advantage of a very wide variety of environments and to populate all regions of the planet by creating and developing various socio-cultures.

Socio-cultures are alive. Socio-cultural change emerges as an extremely complex systemic process that emerges from links between a wide variety of variables. As the loops are numerous and tangled, we can speak of a "chain of chains". Such a process is self-constructed; nobody plans or orders it. We can try to anticipate its evolution but cannot predict it with certainty.

Some socio-cultures are ephemeral. Others last for centuries, not moving far from their equilibrium state until eventually one day they collapse. Others survive by metamorphosing. And humans who participate in the transformations of a socio-culture are usually not aware of it.

Today, with the benefit of hindsight, three hypotheses that contrast with the prevailing pessimism seem to me to stand out.

1. Humanity is being dragged into a process of radical metamorphosis that could lead to a more mature and harmonious phase of its development.

---
[4]. I also want to pay tribute to Edgar Morin, Laurence Baranski and Dr. Robin.

2. Europe is at the forefront of this development and could, if it steers itself intelligently, hasten its emergence, enabling the planet to meet the ecological and geopolitical challenges it faces without undue hardship.

3. This optimism is partly due to the fact that more and more of us are making better use of our brain potentials.

However, a sense of urgency pushed me to write this book. In Europe, in these first decades of the twenty-first century, the crises we are experiencing are avatars of the process of metamorphosis, which is now powerful and well established but does not affect all sectors of our societies equally. The society of ordinary people has already been deeply transformed: its networks and sociosystems are self-organizing, hybrid bodies are emerging within it, beginning to provide regulatory and governance functions. But democracy and bureaucracy as we practice them are transformed laboriously. This persistent time-lag produces poor governance and turbulence. If we do not accelerate the metamorphosis of governance, we risk being unable to wisely manage the geopolitical and ecological crises that threaten us in the relatively short term. Humanity might not recover, or not for a few centuries.

It is the people in all their diversity, ordinary people or leaders, young or old, manual workers and intellectuals, learned and ignorant, women and men, who, through their actions and inactions, fuel the metamorphosis and build the new society of people and its governance. They do it most often without being aware of it, even if they have the intuition that their action is part of a great meaningful movement. Experience has shown me that, when they become aware of an ongoing metamorphosis, when they have some hopeful scenarios in mind, they become more active and more skillful agents of change.

This book, which is methodologically optimistic, and the practice of "happy morphosis", will help develop networks of change agents who will awaken ordinary people and their leaders. I hope that it will promote awareness among the very different people who are contributing to our humanistic metamorphosis, possibly without knowing it.

This book is an abridged and updated version of one written in 2015, which included all the scientific data from research conducted over 60 years, a perspective of the long history of humanity, together with a preface by Alain Berthoz, neurophysicist and honorary professor at the Collège de France.

We start from life and living, which is a complexification of what is physical. Living is not programmed, we cannot rationally predict evolution, which rebounds, which is resilient, which regenerates, in a permanent state of emergent creation.

This is the subject of this deeply humanist book.

Alain de Vulpian

Introduction

"To my grandchildren, co-creators of the future",
who teach me so much.

Travelling over the world for more than fifty years to help businesses and governments better understand their environments, I have always listened to the weak signals that announce change in societies. Day by day they are there around us. But we do not see them. Harvesting them is an exciting exercise. For Cefri (Centre de formation aux réalités internationales / Training Center for International Realities), for which I was responsible, and for SoL (Society for Organizational Learning, issued from MIT), this research was essential. Contacts with the research teams of Cofremca and particularly with Alain de Vulpian helped me a lot. This shared book is the result of respective research that has been able to merge. Anything living creates complexity. Our goal is to make use of this complexity to develop ourselves. The Tower of Babel was "a gift from heaven", and the planet was enriched by diversity; on almost every continent, man has created socio-cultures.

As a historian and a businesswoman seeking to understand in depth human identity and the way it expresses itself through cultures, I was fortunate enough to meet a sociologist who devoted his life to the observation of societies undergoing transformation. Two life experiences thus came together, both looking for keys to interpret human behavior.

Today, through my work with Alain de Vulpian, I have become aware of the gap between the rational education received from our great-grandparents and our parents, and the lives of our own children and grandchildren, wide open to the world. Life today appeals to other aspects of our personalities: the importance of sensory, emotional-relational and spiritual perceptions. We are at a junction point of civilization.

Many people have the impression that the human species is in danger of disappearing. *Homo Sapiens* is a living organism, with all the characteristic drives: to survive, to reproduce and blossom. Facing life, facing death, HS creates socio-cultures that adapt and flourish, allowing him to populate the entire earth.

This point is covered in our first part. To achieve it throughout his short history, HS has continuously metamorphosed: the second part of this work will take us from hunter-gatherers to the modern age, with a particular focus on European metamorphoses. Today we are facing another major fork in the road, which will be covered in part three: will the deified extrapolations of a rational scientific outlook and the persistence of earlier power structures lead us to a dead end, with humanism disappearing? Or shall we take the alternative road of humanistic metamorphosis and the search for meaning and cooperation? Along the way, we shall be exploring the positive seeds of this happy metamorphosis in which you yourself are a participant, and which is leading us to a growing feeling of a change of era.

Irène Dupoux-Couturier

HAPPYMORPHOSE

Part I
Homo Sapiens

The aim of this book is to help the reader understand the deep transformation our society is undergoing that is perceivable around the world and which, beyond its deceptive appearances, signals a "humanist metamorphosis" we must cherish and protect. Who or what is *Homo Sapiens*? In order to be able to talk about the future and survival of our species on a planet dominated by science and technology, we have to examine its deeper nature and its possible evolution. In an increasingly complex and vibrant society, can Homo Sapiens be reinventing himself?

Chapter 1.
Living systems

Who are we? Where do we come from? Where are we going? What is our place in nature? Most human societies, faced with their anxieties, have asked themselves such questions. The cave painters of Lascaux, like the builders of megaliths, the Maya civilization, the Egyptians of the Pharaohs, the early Romans and many others. In response, they invented gods, stories, visions and myths, images of nature, man and woman that gave meaning to their lives and helped them maintain their balance and characterized their socio-cultures.

In many archaic or ancient societies, within everlasting great religions such as Hinduism or Buddhism, man and woman feel immersed in nature and its cycles just as animals do. This has not been the case for our Christianized European ancestors. In the agricultural landscape of the Middle East, Jewish and Christian monotheism allowed for other representations.

Men felt empowered over nature. They invented gods in the image of humans yet more powerful. The Greeks, the Romans and ourselves in their wake, no longer considering the future as deriving from the sequential chains of life, approached and transmitted each other the story of the past as being that of great men and their accomplishments. Fed on the Bible, Man saw himself as a being created by an all-powerful God in his image, a

God who called on Man to dominate nature, even if the biblical words are "to be the steward", "to take care"...

In Europe, the spirit of adventure and conquest pushed our ancestors to explore the world. The "great discoveries" (of southern Africa, America, the Far East) and the intense competition between Portugal, Spain, France and England led to colonization, thus ensuring European hegemony over the rest of the world. The successes of rational thought, scientific investigation and the industrial revolution have enabled Europeans, without breaking completely with the Biblical myth, to conceive of themselves as masters of Nature and bearers of Progress and civilization. Their feeling of sovereignty was strengthened.

FROM DIVINE PLAN TO THE DARWINIAN REVOLUTION

The major upheaval occurred in 1859 with the publication by Charles Darwin of his great book The Origin of Species. Hitherto species had been seen as unchanging, just as God had created them. From then on it became obvious that they resulted from transformation, emanating from each other. Darwin showed that evolution is not directed by a divine design but by natural selection.

After a few defensive skirmishes, the theory of evolution was accepted by the scientific community. Throughout the twentieth century, it would gradually mark the thought of successive generations. In a modified form, Darwin's scientific discovery remains today one of the pillars of modern biology.

THE PRISM OF LIVING

Participants in nature, we are not the masters. Living among the living, we are not cut off from our animality. We now know ourselves to be genetically very close to other mammals. Empathy enables us to communicate with many of them. Ethologists and primatologists[5] show the presence of emotions, movements of empathy and even cultural transmissions in great apes, cetaceans and elephants as it stands for us.

Our brain, as we are beginning to discover, is similar to theirs, but its greater complexity allows us to believe ourselves superior and feel responsible.

New representations of ourselves are thus emerging. They bring us closer to other animals and reintegrate us into Nature, of which we can no longer consider ourselves as the sovereign masters of the creation. It commits ourselves to look at the universe through the prism of living experience.

It is through distorting glasses and prisms that humans look at and understand the universe. Here, the prism is called the ancestors, there it is the gods; elsewhere, it is God and the Devil. One of the main prisms of Europeans was Reason, rational analysis, and what Edgar Morin calls the "simplification principle".[6] Nowadays, a new prism is taking shape which seems to be structured around notions of life and complexity. This radical change is being brought about by the encounter between the development of the life sciences and the transformation of the personality and experiences of Europeans. For minds shaped by rationalist thought, the principle of simplification and the

---

5. Frans de Waal, *Age of empathy, Lessons from nature for a society of solidarity*, Paris, ed. The Links that Liberate, 2010.
6. Edgar Morin, *The method*, Paris, Threshold, 2008.

triumph of the natural sciences, life is a notion that is not easy to incorporate. Life was not created, it has emerged.

Life appears to us as made of matter, and yet, by its organization, differs from it radically. Matter, the physical universe, is continuously degraded (entropy principle), while life resists time, produces order from disorder and categorizes itself, becoming more complex, ever complexifying.

Despite its surprising and strange nature, the paradigm of what is "the Living" began to impregnate the intuition of our contemporaries, if not their clear awareness, from the end of the second third of the twentieth century. Europeans are starting to look at and/or feel the world and the reality around them as living entities. Many in-depth interviews testify to this[7]. Systems and living organisms are complex entities.

Using the energy of the sun directly or indirectly, they act constantly in order to maintain their integrity and identity (homeostasis). They tend to maintain their internal environment and their physiological parameters constant and balanced despite external constraints and events in their environment. But if they cannot, they may break up or jump to a higher level of complexity, and metamorphose.

Take the example of the caterpillar. Having eaten too many leaves, it cannot move anymore. It is going to die and encloses itself in a cocoon. Cells then interconnect to create the imago, or adult stage of the caterpillar, together with what is lacking in the caterpillar, the butterfly's wings.

---

[7]. See Alain de Vulpian, *Listening to ordinary people*, Paris, Dunod, 2003.

Living systems

Living systems and organisms recreate themselves continuously by interacting with their environment; they maintain their structure and orientation despite changes in components. They are autopoietic[8] in the sense that they are self-generated. They self-organize and self-regulate, constantly renewing themselves in such a way that their structure and identity remain coherent. Although they have organs of observation, analysis and decision, the cell and the multicellular organism are both governed in a highly decentralized way.

The emergent factors they produce emanate from internal interactions and not from an overall governing body. In living structures everything is in movement: even stable situations result from movements which, in combination, maintain a balance.

Life was built and builds itself by aggregating and organizing simpler pre-existing elements, both living and non-living. Cells formed from aggregates of cooperating bacteria, a process that produced Sapiens, with its big brain and the capacity to combine humans into clans, bands, tribes, nations, empires, movements, networks, socio-cultures, civilizations, etc.

Contrary to what Europeans believed in Darwin's time, life is made much more by cooperation than conflict and conquest.

Life is fragile and robust at the same time. The living persists in persisting. The living organism reproduces itself. It fights against death but uses it to continue the journey: individual death prolongs collective life. Animals and plants die and are replaced by their descendants.

---

8. Francisco Varela, biologist and philosopher, 1946-2001. *Autonomy and Knowledge*, Paris, Seuil, 1989.

Species or socio-cultures disappear, leaving others to develop. On a different scale, some of our cells decide to die to make room for others that will make life better.

The predominance of the paradigm of life thus marks the consciousness and subconsciousness, postures, mental models and behaviors of ordinary people and many political and economic leaders. Their way of perceiving the world is changing: where they once saw things, events, isolated facts, cause-and-effect links, our contemporaries are more and more likely to see sequences, interactions, systems and ecosystems. Where they once saw stability, they now tend to see more or less stable equilibria. A growing number of tomorrow's leaders grasp complexity and the dynamic in an intuitive way, without intellectualizing: they sense the potentials, the emergences, the tendencies.

LIVING SYSTEMS ARE SUBJECT TO BIFURCATIONS

Westerners believed in foresight and voluntarism. They are beginning to feel that they have to say farewell to these comfortable beliefs.

In the living world as our contemporaries are beginning to perceive it, we are losing the ability to predict. Living systems evolve according to trends that humans may be able to glimpse, but these trends remain uncertain. Ilya Prigogine was awarded the Nobel Prize in Chemistry in 1977 for his theory of dissipative systems. By publishing a book with Isabelle Stengers accessible to non-specialists, it helps us to understand the logic of living systems[9].

---
9. Ilya Prigogine and Isabelle Stengers, *The New Alliance*, Paris, Gallimard, 1979.

Unlike living systems, systems close to their point of equilibrium (for example a sun and its planets) evolve over time in a trajectory that, if we have the necessary information, can be precisely predicted (with a very low probability of error).

On the contrary, living systems develop in time according to a different logic: their future is neither predictable nor predetermined. They have no trajectory. Prigogine shows that their development over time is marked:

- on the one hand, by major trends which are very difficult to deviate, even by applying enormous force,
- on the other hand, living systems experience *bifurcations*: When a system has reached a bifurcation point, a seemingly minor event, a microscopic fluctuation (Edward Lorenz evokes a flutter of butterfly wings in this respect), can have a macroscopic effect by steering the system in a new direction.

We cannot predict the evolution of living organisms and systems. At the most we can perceive trends and cautiously anticipate developments by remaining on the lookout for possible bifurcations.

Similarly, in the living world the comfortable feeling of control that characterized the mechanical world no longer exists. An external will cannot control the evolution of a living system or organism. In response to any deliberate intervention, the living system reacts in its own way. It is autonomous. Its reaction may be in accordance with the intention of the person acting on it, or contradictory, or have nothing to do with it. The living interferes with the living but cannot control it. Humans may be able, to a limited extent, to try to influence the evolutions of a living system, by trying to understand or to feel the main interactions that underlie its functioning, to know its shaping trends and spot weak signals that may indicate possible future bifurcations. And, if they intervene, they have to be on the lookout for the system's reactions in order to adjust their intervention: their attitude must be tentative, searching.

A proactive intervention may have no effect: the body absorbs, compensates and preserves its homeostasis and autopoiesis. Antonio Damasio[10] defines three characteristics of life: survival, reproduction, fulfilment. Varela emphasizes the capacity of the living creature to self-regenerate in response to environmental change; this is autopoiesis, which may produce an opposite reaction to what was sought by intervention, resulting in turbulence and perverse effects. Intervention may also provoke a desired reaction, but one which in turn will provoke new reactions, sequences of sequences, escaping the control of the deliberate change agent.

This devaluation of forecasting and control affects not only the collective intelligence of ordinary people but also the mental models of a growing number of leaders, sometimes as a vague intuition, sometimes as clear conviction. In companies, for example, tentative "tinkering" strategies (in the words of François Jacob[11]) tend to replace logical planning.

Self-organized living systems are stronger and more efficient than systems rationally organized from above;

---

10. Antonio Damasio, *The Strange Order of Things, life, feeling and the making of cultures*, Penguin Random House, 2017.
11. François Jacob, *La logique du vivant : une histoire de l'hérédité*, Paris, Gallimard, 1976.

they are more effective, more energy efficient, and less polluting than mechanical systems.

Living structures are not planned or controlled, but perhaps they can be cultivated, influenced, redirected. Our contemporaries are beginning to dream of other forms of piloting, derived from an understanding of living systems.

BIFURCATION TODAY: UNCERTAINTIES AND RETURN TO BEING HUMAN

Besides the loss of certainty in our mastery and sovereignty, a deep disillusionment has gradually invaded the minds of Europeans and Americans. It was further tinged with anxiety at the beginning of the twenty-first century.

A void appeared: The regal and reassuring Newtonian science of the nineteenth century moved into an age of uncertainty, a quantum world beyond our comprehension.

Consequently, the great structuring ideologies of the twentieth century - nationalism, socialism, communism, fascism - have all lost their power to blind us with uncritical conviction.

And, a little later still, the fascination of modernity and the race for consumption has also begun to dissipate. An ecological perception of the human condition has gradually been affirmed.

Ecology, which is concerned with the health of the biosphere - that is to say the living Earth - emerged as a scientific discipline in the last third of the nineteenth century, very shortly after the publication of the work of Darwin. But this birth did not shake the scientific community or make any impression on the collective consciousness. Awareness was slow to develop.

The Club of Rome was formed in 1968 and its first report, "Stop the Growth", was published in 1972. Ecology remained very much a minority concern. It was not until the first decade of the twenty-first century that a powerful wave of collective emotion led to a massive increase in awareness.

The Earth with its plants, animals, humans and their various activities, seems to us to constitute a living mega-system[12], but one whose human activities dangerously threaten the equilibrium of the whole.

Perhaps the Earth, with its biosphere, its rocks, its gases, its chemical exchanges and its history, can be considered a living organism, one that could react to correct an exaggerated development of the human species. We feel, in fact, that humanity faces major threats in the twenty-first century.

We are worried, not only because the power and status of Europe and the West are being shaken by the current restructuring of the world. We are worried above all because we have (at last!) understood that our technical and industrial development over the last two centuries and its transmission to the world at large have transformed our environment in such a way that the survival of our civilization and our species is now threatened.

Today, our European past seems less glorious than we had thought. We went astray, failing to realize that our "progress" could have perverse effects. And so we have ended up overpopulating the Earth.

---

12. James Lovelock, Gaia, A New Look at Life on Earth, Oxford University Press, 1979.

The forms of development that we have invented deplete its resources, disrupt its climates and cause the extinction of many species. We have destroyed civilizations. Our laboratories and our arsenals have produced weapons so devastating that they could eliminate mankind, or even life on Earth. Contrary to the claims of our ideologies, it does not seem that we have made the human race more fulfilled or less violent.

In the early 1980s, observatories of socio-cultural change in France and the United States[13] described this void and reported that a feeling of loss or lack of meaning was spreading massively among our populations.

The quest for meaning became a major current on both sides of the Atlantic. More and more ordinary people embarked on a quest for meaning that continues today. Some people looked for situations in their personal life, at work, or as citizens, to make them feel that their existence made sense. Others, often ideologically syncretic, explored ancient wisdoms and, for example, became attracted by Buddhism or practiced yoga or were interested in shamanism (see Chapter 4), or all of the above. Others joined sects or fundamentalist movements.

Return to being human

This quest for meaning leads to an interrogation of oneself and the human species. Many of our contemporaries are vaguely aware that it is their minds and brains that drive both evolutionary success and the errors of Homo Sapiens.

---

13. Cofremca in France, SRI in the United States.

Seekers are encouraged to deepen the internal dialogue with their mind and their central nervous system and to try to act on them.

Our questions about the role of the human species and its responsibilities towards the future of life are crossing new thresholds. Does our big brain make us the spearhead of a certain form of evolution that is poised to emerge as the next link in the chain?

Will our role be to disappear and give way to other, better-equipped life forms than ours? To contribute to the emergence of another socio-culture, perhaps one that marks the beginning of a happier and more fulfilling phase of the species' progress on Earth. Can we help ensure that evolution continues without major disasters and leads to a more harmonious socio-culture?

We have become aware of our limits. We have understood that our short-sighted actions often triggered catastrophic effects, that the mythical images of Nature and Humanity we had built had fueled our predatory and improvident behaviors, as well as our remarkable provisional material successes. We are beginning to wonder if we are not congenitally doomed to this form of blindness. But this awareness, a possible outline of a new wisdom, encourages us to be vigilant and to extend our ability to really influence the course of events. We wonder if our brain does not have potentials that we are not aware of, that we could develop and would make us wiser and more astute. We also wonder if other dimensions of reality, which would have been neglected by Western rational thought, could provide possibilities of intervention and thus contribute to giving new meaning to our existence.

Chapter 2. Understanding the metamorphoses of Homo Sapiens

HOMO SAPIENS IS A SOCIO-CULTURAL ANIMAL

The human species is very young and evolves very quickly. After its release from Africa, it has dramatically changed in the last 50 millennia: the human population living on Earth has increased from a few thousand to seven billion and soon nine billion people; life expectancy has increased, multiplied by three or four; intellectual and artistic productions have been fabulous; the capacity to manage the complexity generated by this progression has been ensured. Despite famines and wars, life has continued.

In 50,000 years, Homo Sapiens has populated the entire Earth. Unlike most living species that can survive only in a particular environment - their biotope - Sapiens has invented ways of living and exploiting the environment - socio-cultures - allowing him to adapt to all regions and all climates of the Earth (except Antarctica). The evolution from the ancestor of the chimpanzee to the first Homo was genetic and relatively slow: 7 million years until the appearance of Homo Sapiens; the evolution of Sapiens is mainly socio-cultural and fast, probably within 300,000 years. The ability to develop socio-cultures appears to be a fundamental human characteristic. We call socio-culture all the interactive characters (livelihoods, personality traits, technical know-how and skills, habits, beliefs, demographic regimes, habitat types, etc.) that enable a population to survive in a sustainable way in a given environment.

Our evolution is embodied in extremely diverse socio-cultures. Some are ephemeral. Others last for centuries, moving away from their equilibrium state and eventually collapsing. Others survive by metamorphosing.

Socio-cultures are living structures. Socio-cultural development emerges through an extremely complex systemic process arising from links between a wide variety of variables. Such a process is self-constructed (Varela). Nobody plans or controls it. It may be directed by extremely persistent shaping trends, but these are always likely to bifurcate (Prigogine). We can try to anticipate their evolution but cannot predict this with certainty.

The success of Sapiens is largely due to the fact that it is a socio-cultural animal that is both extremely inventive, but not sufficiently farsighted in its appreciation of the future. Homo Sapiens is not equipped to deliberately build socio-cultures or to consciously control their evolution. But, without being clearly aware of it, it adopts emerging socio-cultures, accompanies their development and their complexification and, if possible, uses them to prolong life.

By trying to lead their lives well and face the challenges they encounter, by trying to save their skin or increase their well-being, humans fuel socio-cultural change. But, most often, they do not steer their socio-cultures. For example,

Homo Sapiens, in peril of death without the protection of the forests, deploys prodigious ingenuity, though he may not be aware of the socio-cultural significance of these actions. When men and women choose to work in the fields, joining a team that is an incipient agricultural village, a major socio-cultural evolution begins. Its continuation will lead to the establishment of specializations, hierarchy, domestication of men, etc.

We learn about it afterwards. But neither the team's "big men" nor their collaborators know at the time that they are building the future.

They choose their behavior because it is good for them, it responds to their tropisms and impulses. The direction the process is taking is not visible or even defined at the beginning, only taking shape along the way. Perhaps, a few generations later, some will be aware of the evolution in progress, will more or less identify the trend under way and seek more or less consciously to strengthen it or, if there is still time, to redirect it. In rare cases, perhaps, the early intuition of certain individuals or populations feeds the nascent movement.

This limited socio-cultural competence seems to be linked to certain features of our central nervous system and the functioning of the human species, characteristics which we should better understand in order to strengthen them.

The human brain creates socio-cultures adapted to its environment

First and foremost, it is the extreme adaptability of his brain that makes man a sociocultural animal.

The hunter of mammoths and small game during the Chauvet cave period, the workman building pyramids or canals, the Egyptian scribe, the Aztec warrior, the Roman citizen, the good Western consumer or the Viennese bourgeois described by Freud all have the same brains, but brains whose synaptic patterns and/or interplay of neuromediators differ. They use the potentials of their brain differently.

Great apes are very close to us. Our brains are similar but very different. Ours is much bigger (as was Neanderthal man's). Its complexity is extraordinary: each one of our 100 billion neurons is connected to thousands of synapses.

This complexity is such that it is inconceivable for the detailed development of the brain to be programmed genetically: it self-organizes according to the interactions between a genetic program and circumstances. Not everything is predetermined by the genome; experience along the way contributes to the organization of the brain. Because of this complexity and its unplanned self-organization, the diversity of possibilities is infinite.

Our brains do not use all their potential. In any given socio-culture, brains use some potentials, but may use others in another socio-culture. We have no knowledge of the extent or diversity of potentials that could be actualized by the human brain. An emerging socio-culture could develop alongside brain potentials that have not yet been activated. It is also likely that hunter-gatherers were taking advantage of some potential in the human brain that today we have paralyzed. And conversely.

Human offspring are born with brains that are unfinished. At puberty, the brain is four times larger than it was at birth, while the little chimpanzee is born with a brain that is physically almost complete. A baby produces around 25,000 neurons per second. This means that the human brain is being constructed in a socio-cultural context, interacting with parents who belong to a certain milieu, who have a particular personality, motivations, customs, religion, who speak a certain language. According to processes that neuroscience is just beginning to discover, all these features will leave strong and lasting influences on the child's brain. It will be, to a large extent, marked by the socio-culture and the environment into which it was born. It will be all the more a child of its parents' socio-culture and their environment given that many societies organize very elaborate educational paths to ensure the conformity of young people to the desired model. But sometimes circumstances are such that children deviate more or less strongly from the parental pattern: successive generations that are not carbon copies of those preceding are powerful factors of socio-cultural evolution.

The plasticity of the brain is not limited to childhood and adolescence. According to developing neuroscience[14], the brain remains extremely plastic throughout life.

Connections that are used or more used are reinforced while those that are less used become weaker. The brain is marked by its past, but new experiences transform it.

This malleability allows very different types of brains to exist in large groups that coexist or succeed each other. For example, socio-cultures have shaped the brains of a majority of humans into slaves, disciplined mobs, savage warriors or relatively autonomous individuals, and the brains of a few into leaders, scribes, priests or adventurous

---

14. See for example, Antonio Damasio, *Self comes to mind, constructing the conscious brain*, Pantheon, 2010.

innovators. Chance events and interactions can allow some brains to escape the mold and innovate.

HOMO SAPIENS IS A SOCIAL ANIMAL THAT LIVES IN NETWORKS

The human brain is tuned to "otherness"

Society does not emerge as the result of a contract between individuals. It is a first datum. It is part of human nature. In the savannah, the individual hunter-gatherer is too weak and helpless against lions and tigers to survive for long. He has a vital need for the solidarity and collective intelligence of his group to defend or shelter himself and to hunt. Mankind survived as a species only because it is biologically part of a society. The child learns to speak only in interactions with his fellow creatures, and his brain develops properly only in society.

From observation of the brains of our contemporaries, the neurosciences teach us that our central nervous system is well equipped to drive our interpersonal and social relationships. With his big brain man can adjust to his fellow creatures, create a social environment and operate among the complexities of a living society.

Empathy - the capacity to feel in oneself and possibly to share the emotions and the feelings of the other person, even to imagine his state of mind and his intentions - is even more developed in us than in the mammals closest to us. Neurologists tell us that we make "theories of the mind" of the other and orient our interactions accordingly. Shared empathy undoubtedly plays a vital role in human communications and in communication between humans and certain animals.

Relying on this empathy, we spend our time producing future scenarios: "If I do this, they will react like that and then..." We look ahead and our empathic intuition is often accurate, giving us a certain capacity for interpersonal and social anticipation. But we are sure of nothing. We store kinds of "memories of the future" that help guide our actions without dissipating our fear of the future. In all socio-cultures, we look for help to see the future and make it more favorable: shamans, Yi King, oracles, prophets, protective gods, astrologers, futurists.

Developing neuroscience is beginning to glimpse one of the neural underpinnings of empathy. In 1996, an Italian neurologist, Giacomo Rizzolatti and his team from the University of Parma, discovered the existence of mirror neurons[15]. Active in macaque and other monkeys, they are particularly developed in humans. If I make a move, if I perform an action, some neurons in my motor cortex are activated and if you watch me do this, the same neurons in your motor cortex are activated. The connection is direct and does not seem to have to go through systems of intellectual representation. This fundamental discovery about human-to-human connections no doubt opens the way for many others.

Our brains co-produce collective phenomena

If we judge by what ethnologists have learned from surviving hunter-gatherers they have observed during the twentieth century, brains within a group or clan have a tendency to harmonize in a sort of collective intelligence or emotion.

---

15. Giacomo Rizzolatti and Corrado Sinigaglia, The mirror neuron system, NCBI, PubMed, US National Library of Medicine, 2009.

This harmonization may be facilitated by certain rites or the intervention of a shaman.

In historical societies the population tends to share the same beliefs and stories, quite distinct from those shared by another population. Similarly, collective emotions are common.

These can have a devastatingly contagious force. Individuals are embroiled in crowds, mass movements, waves of opinion or emotion. Burn a witch or scapegoat, exterminate the enemy, glorify a hero; hunger riots, religious wars. Reversals of public opinion or waves of emotion brutally affect entire populations. In equality-oriented societies, these movements are often generated by the individuals themselves: they are facilitated by deep conversations, group discussions, initiatory rites, trances. In hierarchical societies, movements are often generated from top to bottom by charismatic leaders and orchestrated by impressive ceremonies.

Our brains seem to tend to vibrate together, to vibrate in tune with those we feel close to or people around us. Are mirror neurons involved in these co-vibrations? We consider telepathies from unconscious to unconscious. Neuroscience is slow in providing us with solid answers.

Contactless connections

By examining the evolution of the human species from socio-culture to socio-culture, we see the same emergences and the same phase evolutions being repeated. For example, livestock farming and agriculture emerge in different places. Humanity has reinvented the state several times and anthropologists evoke the "first states" - those states that were settled at different times on different continents and without any contact between the populations that gave birth to them. Similarly, myths reappear in socio-cultures far apart in space and/or time without one having copied the other.

These similarities remain partly mysterious. They are the manifestation of the fact that the human species is a living super-organism that evolves in interaction with its terrestrial environment. Within this living super-organism that is humanity, the position of individual humans is analogous to that of the cells within the organism that each of us is.

These similarities could be traces of very old memories of humanity. They could also reveal some common traits of the human mind reacting similarly to similar circumstances. But they could also be the symptoms of strange communications between contactless brains. This last possibility has given rise in the twentieth century to various hypotheses that twenty-first century research will probably confirm or refute.

For example, Carl Gustav Jung, one of the fathers of psychoanalysis, evokes what he called the collective unconscious, that is, the transpersonal part of the unconscious psyche that permeates all human history in whatever eras or places, and which would influence and condition individual and group representations. The British biologist Rupert Sheldrake has put forward a theory of "morphic fields" and "formative causation" explaining that a phenomenon that has once occurred has a tendency to reoccur.

Reflecting on communication without connections between brains, other researchers have considered an analogy with quantum mechanics. In the microscopic world of atoms and elementary particles, when two particles collide, they give rise to two new particles which, even if far apart from one another in space and time, behave as if they were joined by an invisible link. They envision that the same could happen in neural networks. This rapid glance at living systems and the place of Homo Sapiens will enable us to better understand its socio-cultural developments and the metamorphoses it has continuously experienced.

HAPPYMORPHOSE

Part II
The socio-cultural metamorphoses of Homo Sapiens

Throughout its short history, Homo Sapiens has constantly metamorphosed to adapt to changing environments. To survive, it has created socio-cultures. Understanding these evolutions, these metamorphoses, allows us to better perceive the bifurcation facing us today. The rapid study of these socio-cultures[16] will illustrate the characteristics of each of them: the era of survival and cooperation; the era of the discovery of agriculture and livestock; the era of civilizations and competition; and, today, the gestation of a new era whose shaping trends we will try to perceive. We will place particular emphasis on the two earlier European metamorphoses as they are at the base of the current on-going planetary metamorphosis.

---

16. Alain de Vulpian, *Éloge de la métamorphose: en marche vers une nouvelle humanité*, grand prix de l'essai Académie française, 2016.

Chapter 3.
From hunter-gatherers to the age of civilizations

Through the observation of the flow of socio-cultures, kinships and phases can be perceived. At certain times, different societies, without contacts between them, are marked by identical tendencies or make innovations that are similar and meaningful. As time goes by, socio-cultures seem to become more complex and involve populations that are more and more diverse.

Observing the flow of sociocultures that occurred over the last 50 millennia, through a prism that blurs differences and anomalies in order to shed light on the metamorphosis in which we are currently involved, four phases can be considered

The first phase, that of nomadic hunter-gatherers, is the longest. It has undoubtedly profoundly affected the organization of our brain. In very different, possibly surprising and often dangerous environments, these men and women learn to survive, then to live better, to collaborate in small groups with little specialization and probably no permanent hierarchies. They cultivate their alliance with nature and its spirits. They build up their ingenuity, their empathy, their autonomy. Every day, everyone has to deploy all his energy, all his human capacities to react to the unexpected. We have potentially inherited this vitality and these remarkable skills.

But, ten or twelve thousand years ago, with the help of global warming, a phase of transition occurred that transformed in just a few thousand years, the majority of nomadic hunter-gatherers into sedentary villagers, that learned how to cultivate land and plants and how to domesticate animals. They discovered hard work, storage, property, theft, a beginning of specialization and hierarchy. They gave birth to more children and learned to live in larger groups. The relationship of the human species to the planet Earth changed profoundly: the species Homo took possession of nature and sought to dominate it.

It was Sumer, between the Tigris and the Euphrates, that around 4,000 BC inaugurated the next phase of human development: the era of civilizations. These emerged in the basins of other large rivers (Indus, Nile, Yellow River), where conditions were particularly favorable for agriculture and livestock. Building on the discoveries and achievements of the previous phase, these self-organizing civilizations had common characteristics: they built cities, developed writing, practiced trade. They established hierarchies and more or less despotic states. They created religions - often state-run - to give meaning to life, contribute to social cohesion, and strengthen the ruler. They made war a common practice. In addition to plants and animals, they domesticated men and women, educating them according to predefined models.

Here we see the emergence of similar pathways and major innovations that will mark the future of human history. A new socio-cultural field profoundly different from the previous two was to mark the history of the kingdoms, empires and nations that would settle the Earth over the next millennia.

Most civilized societies have a pyramidal structure: they teach their children obedience, hierarchical mimicry and conformity to dominant patterns, and educate children of the elite so that they find their place in a society they dominate

On the other hand, many hunter-gatherer societies that operate on a level-playing field ensure that forms of education are established to develop initiative, autonomy, the ability to find one's own path, and personal choice of models to imitate.

In most bands and clans of hunter-gatherers, it is essential for effective self-regulation that the empathy of all their members be well developed.

On the other hand, a hierarchical society that maintains the status of its plebeians or its army will seek to paralyze the development of empathy since it makes people socially adept and protects them from indoctrination.

To select suitable forms of personality, in its sedentary and hierarchical phase, humanity has domesticated men and women, inventing a very effective system of social reproduction and shaping of personalities. The couple has been institutionalized to educate their children and, at the same time, the selection of mates is controlled so that they belong to the same caste, the same order, the same social class, the same milieu. To better maintain homeostasis, many socio-cultures have supplemented this system with very elaborate educational programs and different forms of suitable codes of conduct.

Part II. The socio-cultural metamorphoses of Homo Sapiens

These socio-cultures were deliberately constructed neither by the peoples, nor by kings, nor by gods. They did not emulate models that did not exist yet. They emerged from similar concatenations of chains within living societies. These socio-cultures have emerged around the world.

In this book, we will study in particular the characteristics of metamorphoses in the European and Western socio-cultures because they are at the origin of the current metamorphosis extending today to the whole planet. It is the society in which we live today, with all its question marks and its huge potentialities. What we can perceive today has been brought to light by 60 years of anthropo-sociological research, in particular at Cofremca-Sociovision.

Chapter 4.
European metamorphoses

In the 1930s, the German sociologist Norbert Elias[17] undertook a monumental historical research into the evolution that led Europeans countries evolve from the Middle Ages to the present day: the birth of the state and self-controlled rational elites, sociogenesis and psychogenesis.

Wondering about the origins of their culture, many Europeans see them in Greece or Rome, the birth of Christ or the Enlightenment.

However, Norbert Elias tells us, "It is impossible to go back to the origins of a process that does not have origins. Wherever one begins, everything is in movement and the continuation of a previous stage… let us take the medieval level as our point of departure and examine the movement, the evolutionary curve that has led to the modern situation."

Europe has experienced two metamorphoses: the one described by Elias as a "process of civilization", characterized by the Renaissance and the rise of modern society, and the one in which we live today, characterized by a radical change in people's behavioral characteristics. At the turn of the twentieth and twenty-first centuries, we are at the heart of this second metamorphosis.

---

17. Norbert Elias, *Über den Prozess der Zivilisation*, 1939.

Part II. The socio-cultural metamorphoses of Homo Sapiens

FIRST METAMORPHOSIS: THE RENAISSANCE AND THE ERA OF RATIONALITY

From the feudal age to modern society, our European civilization has metamorphosed extensively. It is in many of its aspects a civilization like the others. It has most of the socio-cultural characteristics of civilizations in general: writing, states, wars, commerce, hierarchy, bureaucracy, domestication of man, etc.

But Europe cultivated rational and intellectual intelligence among its elites to a point that had hitherto never been reached, and suspended the use of sensory, emotional-relational and spiritual perceptions.

This culture of rationality has led us to develop a science of things, techniques, industry and war machines of such a prodigious efficiency, that it marks a break with other civilizations. Europe thus has developed an unparalleled power over nature and the rest of the world, feeding a strong population growth which, in spite of the demographic disasters of the fourteenth century (Hundred Years' War, epidemics of plague, famines), rose from 50 million in 1200 to over 500 million in 1950. The extent of this metamorphosis parallels what many socio-cultures experienced in the Neolithic.

In Europe, our elites have organized our society, our businesses, our democratic or totalitarian governance systems, and our international relations in a rational way. We have built a rational economy whose development we have been unable to steer, and which is now out of control. From crisis to crisis it has fueled international conflicts and class struggle. In the twentieth century we reached a dead end: totalitarian nation-states, two world wars, tens of millions of deaths, the Holocaust, weapons capable of destroying the planet. Finally, we have come to understand that our industrial and demographic development is causing planet-wide disruption and climate change, exhausting the world's resources and upsetting the ecosystem on which depends the survival of our species. In two words, a species in the process of committing suicide.

SECOND METAMORPHOSIS: 20TH-21ST CENTURIES, FLOURISHING PERSONALISM

Advances in neuroscience have helped us understand that in the complexity of life, humans are unable to behave properly if they use only their rational brain without the collaboration of their emotional brain[18].

After four centuries of metamorphosis, by the late nineteenth and early twentieth centuries, Europeans looked at the world and at each other through a sophisticated rational filter, their culture leading to rationalized, literate, ideologized individuals, deaf to their feelings, emotions, intuitions and impulses. They were conditioned and manipulated without suspecting it. They easily felt themselves members of groups and classes, nationalists, proletarians and, for a small number, already a consumers' society.

Today, more and more "ordinary people"[19] - who are still equipped with a well-developed rational intelligence - are combining it with an emotional-relational intelligence that looks ahead and self-guides. Their reason analyzes their

---

18. Antonio Damasio, *Descartes' error, emotion, reason and the human brain"*, 1995.
19. Alain de Vulpian, *Towards the third modernity, How ordinary people are transforming the world*, Triarchy Press, 2008.

emotions, their impulses, their flashes of empathy, and learns from the development of their relationships.

Individuals become fully-fledged people, free from conventions, packaging and authorities, and gain autonomy. People are equipped to act in a complex society, their social skills progress. And they build, possibly unwittingly or unknowingly, a different society, a different economy and civilization.

Rather than a second metamorphosis, we can consider this episode as the second *phase* of the metamorphosis of European civilization.

Its roots can be found in the emancipatory impulse of happiness and freedom which touched the European intelligentsia early on, with Spinoza and the Age of Enlightenment, even though it did not begin to penetrate the awareness of ordinary people until a few centuries later.

It was at the beginning of the 1950s that sociological field research in the United States, Sweden and France shed light on transformations of personalities and morals foreshadowing a real socio-cultural bifurcation.

A significant proportion of 15- to 25-year-olds spoke for themselves and others in very new terms that set them apart from most of their contemporaries and from their parents' generation. They identified themselves less in terms of categories, labels or ideologies, they spoke less about reasons for their behavior and much more about their feelings, their emotions, their instincts, their personality. Referring to others, they spoke less about their socio-economic characteristics than about their motivations, their inner life, their personality, which they enjoyed discovering through feelings. In Sweden, as in the United States or France, interviews show that this generational break is largely due to a shift a quarter of a century previously in relations and educational climate in the families of these young people.

At the same time, an awareness that had emerged in modern segments of the bourgeoisie and the middle classes in the 1920s and 1930s was spreading: they felt that society which wanted everyone to stay in their place and to respect the rules, the conventions and the authorities was becoming less demanding; more of them felt they could improve their standing and modernity a little and emancipate themselves. But not too fast. In order to manage properly their progress they needed to feel where they stood and where others like them stood. This was the beginning of renewed awareness of intraception and empathy.

Our Four Brains Begin to Dialogue

Young and old alike, Europeans begin to reactivate areas or functions of their brains that were dormant. They become progressively more open to sensory, emotional, empathic, socioperceptive inputs without losing their rationality. Dialogue became the first item on their agenda as they began to perceive that society was manipulating them and realized, for example, the illusory nature of the race for social standing. Thus, Europeans became much more knowledgeable, intuitive, able to anticipate and control their lives autonomously in the growing complexity of society.

During the eighties, it became clear that in just a few decades, millions and then hundreds of millions of adults and young people went through a fabulous self-apprenticeship which, step by step, installed a more open and intimate contact with the various dimensions of their animal vitality. This apprenticeship has made them more capable of reasoning for themselves over their emotions, their lives and their relationships to others and to communities. They are more able also to understand the successes and the disappointments that met their quest for happiness, fulfillment and sense. Having reintegrated the animal into themselves and deepened their rationality, they have become full-fledged people, more autonomous and wiser than their predecessors, less open to manipulation, more capable of building for themselves lives that suit them.

In the late nineteenth and early twentieth centuries, they looked at the world and others through a rational filter. They were rationalized, literate, ideologized individuals, deaf to their feelings, emotions and impulses. They were conditioned and manipulated. They easily felt they belonged to groups, nationalist masses, proletarian masses and, for a small number already, consumer groups. Today ordinary people are multiplying with a highly developed rational intelligence and a bodily, emotional-relational intelligence that progresses and refines itself. Their reason analyzes their emotions, their impulses, their flashes of empathy and learns from the evolution of their relationships. Individuals, capable of behaving in a complex society, become people in their own right. They free themselves from conventions, packaging and authorities, and gain autonomy. Their social skill is progressing.

As part of the same development, men and women have also awoken to an intelligence that could be called spiritual. In the extreme diversity of its socio-cultures, Homo Sapiens has always taken into account a hidden dimension: that of the spirits, the gods, the sky, life before and after death, the future he was trying to guess. The "hyper-rationalist" West had cooled this spiritual impulse, even forbidden it. Now it has re-emerged and has begun to dialogue with the rational mind.

It is likely that in our brains, neural wiring can be organized in various ways. One could say that the grandparents of our interviewees were hooked up to a highly developed rational brain, but that they had kept their emotional-relational and spiritual brains in hibernation. In contrast, the interviewees are connected to all four brains interacting freely with each other, which radically changes their relationship to the world and to others.

Essential supports for the individualistic and hierarchical society of mass consumption have eroded: the docility of easily manipulated individuals, the myth of our superiority and modernity, competition for social standing and hierarchy, codification of economic and social life... A new social fabric is beginning to self-organize.

This bifurcation affects our civilization. It was already visible in the 1950s in Scandinavia, France, the United Kingdom, Switzerland, Belgium, Holland and the United States. It settled with a delay of about ten years in certain countries that had undergone totalitarian regimes, such as Germany, Italy, Spain, and Portugal.

The three decades following the end of the Second World War have been called the "Glorious Thirty". This was for the Euro-American civilization a paradoxical time both in its continuity and its break with the pre-war period. It ensured full employment, dramatically improved standards of living and reduced inequality. It deepened and strengthened democracy. It fostered inter-company and international competition, and exacerbated individual rivalry, but it also reduced the intensity of conflicts between nations and social classes. To a greater or lesser extent planned or liberal, these three decades saw the establishment of a rational, hierarchical and individualistic society of mass consumption in line with what was presaged during the 1920s and 1930s. But in doing so, they generated modes of existence and education that were to nurture the emergence, then the development, of personalities radically different from the all-invasive rationality that had been one of the dominant characteristics of European civilization.

THE CHANGE IN PERSONALITIES: FOUR MAJOR TRANSFORMATIONS

In recent decades, in a society more intensely integrated than ever but where everyday life can be difficult, the transformation of personalities has increased and affects an increasingly large population. Each of these men and women, at their respective levels of maturity, can deepen contact with different parts of their brains (rational, emotional-relational, sensory, spiritual). Each person so equipped seeks to improve his life in his own way within a social fabric that is more and more organic, informal, flexible, complex and quite permissive.

It seems to us that four personality transformations are developing which are promising for the future: explosion of vitality, broadening of rationality, quest for meaning, and finally, strategic opportunism based on a culture of socio-perception.

Explosion of vitality

The 1980s marked the beginning of a period in which many Europeans who had changed profoundly in previous decades relaxed and benefited from their evolution. More and more men and women felt relatively directly in touch with their feelings, their emotions, their intuitions, their drives, but also with their reasoning intelligence. They felt they had grown up and could grow even more.

They overflow with a calm vitality. They like to live, to feel the blood circulating in their arteries. They like to feel competent, to have the impression that they can cope with all situations. Cofremca has described this form of personality as "vital". These vital persons are bio-emotional-intellectual machines that work better than before, that are less stuck, that make better use of their potentials. They like to participate in groups full of vitality that react at the first sign. They prefer biological self-regulation to legal or bureaucratic regulations. They want to do it themselves or be involved in the interactions that drive the systems they are part of. Their dominant motivation is not to win the race, to accumulate possessions, nor to serve this or that ideology, but to optimize their lives and those of their loved ones, or even of humanity.

They are often in situations that encourage them to mobilize all their human potentials to come out with a positive result. This is why some aspects of their personality profiles are more similar to those of a hunter-gatherer facing unforeseen situations, than to a worker building pyramids or a Taylorian skilled workman on his assembly line.

Expansion, opening, deepening of rationality.

During the 1980s, we witnessed the beginning of a massive integration of emotions and reason that can only progress. Openness to our animal instincts and impulses, the focus on sensations, emotions and the expression of one's personality had prompted many Westerners to be wary of reason.

Meanwhile, with the development of secondary and higher education, the ability to reason for oneself had improved for a significant part of the population. In the face of their invasive emotional life and the growing complexity of the organic social fabric, many were confronted by complex problems of vital importance to them: Why is my relationship falling apart? Why are my children fleeing the house? Why have I not reached my goals? What misled me when I misunderstood the reaction of this or that friend? In an attempt to answer these questions, a growing proportion of our contemporaries begin to use their reason to reflect not on clear ideas, concepts, arguments, or ideologies, but on impressions, intuitions, premonitions, concrete experiences and intimacies - theirs, those of others and those of society. They seek systemic sequences rather than causes. These "expanded rationalists" reflect on themselves as actors in life. They thus enter into a kind of apprenticeship, and become, little by little, savvier, a little more capable of steering their lives so as to obtain a little extra happiness and meaning, to maintain the affections that are important to them, to avoid tensions, stresses and conflicts.

The search for meaning

Reflecting on themselves and their lives, they encounter more and more often the problem of the meaning of what they do and the meaning of their lives. They discover that they feel better when what they do makes sense to them. On the rubble of values that came from before and from above (God, the fatherland, the working class, progress, success), many rebuild a personal theory of meaning-for-self from their daily experience. They evaluate their work, their family life, and their loves against the grid of meaning and nonsense. Whatever awakens in me an impression of wholeness or a spiritual emotion is what makes sense to me.

Whatever brings us, our children, our loved ones a lasting well-being and fulfillment makes sense. By extension, what brings fulfillment to the socio-economy as a whole or to the global ecosystem is meaningful. To achieve, each in his own way, the optimization of a situation or participation in the process of interactions that leads to this result is meaningful.

In competitions, our contemporaries prefer co-operation and win-win games. To conformity, they prefer fulfillment. To the acquisition or protection of territories, they prefer the search for favorable situations in processes.

Such insights experienced by people who are in the socio-cultural vanguard could be precursors of personal moralities and new, more or less shared value systems leading to new forms of humanism.

Development of a culture of socio-perception: empathy and intuition

In our fields of research, we see people who behave like opportunistic strategists and succeed quite well in steering their lives astutely. Their profile is schematically the following: In a complex and uncertain environment, they orient themselves by making combined use of their reason, their emotion and their intuition[20]. They cultivate their capacity for empathy, enrich their emotions and thus feel acutely the happiness and suffering of others.

But they keep reasonable control over their outbursts of compassion, not losing sight of their self-oriented central ambition of making a life that suits them fully.

Cultivating empathy helps them to perceive or imagine the representation of themselves that forms in the minds of others with whom they interact. With these "theories of the mind", they anticipate

the behavior and reactions of others and, learning from their mistakes, they improve the relevance of their expectations.

They cultivate their understanding of socio-systems, the way they perceive things boosts the motivations of all that are concerned (people or groups); they anticipate the behaviors and feel the latencies and dynamics that underlie the course of things. They cover the strategic field of the life that is best for them: they are ready at any moment to take advantage of opportunities and threats closest to it.

They dig deeper into their perception of the future. Beginning in the 1980s, we see more young people who tell us that they do not have clear and fixed goals for their lives, but that they consistently keeping an eye on the way the future is emerging and how they could use it to improve their lives.

---

20. The neurologist Antonio Damasio has shown that humans only retain the ability to pilot their lives wisely if the rational and emotional areas of the brain work together. See his book op. cit.

They are ready to adjust their new goals to these shifts in perspective. This human capacity to treat the future as a store of scenarios and trends, with hypotheses of action to be taken, was probably fundamental to the survival of the species. It was abandoned by a culture whose narrow rationalism was stifling to wider perceptions, but the metamorphosis now under way is reawakening the sleeping princess.

Uniting emotion and reason, deepening their empathy and their intelligence of socio-systems, these strategic opportunists improve their intelligence of the future. They become more socio-perceptive, that is to say more apt than previous generations to perceive chains of sequences, to identify weak signals announcing blockages, fluctuations or bifurcations, to consider the possible impacts of their actions on their happiness and scenarios of the future. They are beginning to be well equipped to lead their lives wisely, in a society where individual behavior and relationships become freer and less controlled by conventions or authorities.

When they are involved in socio-systems where camps or interests are opposed, they tend to look far ahead and seek the common good rather than the victory of a particular camp.

Faced with a complex socio-system, the socioperceptives that we see at work do not seek to analyze it in its micro-details. They embrace it as a totality and manage to feel among its dynamics those that have a strategic impact on their field of action. Their mental processes are reminiscent of what Alain Berthoz calls simplexity[21].

---

21. Alain Berthoz, *La Simplexité*, Odile Jacob, 2009.

Part II. The socio-cultural metamorphoses of Homo Sapiens

This neurologist considers simplexity to be one of the most remarkable inventions of living experience, one which allows a quick response to extremely complex situations, taking into account past experience and anticipating possible futures in order to simultaneously perceive what is essential, and to act in the same instant.

Simplified diagram of the process of generating socio-perception

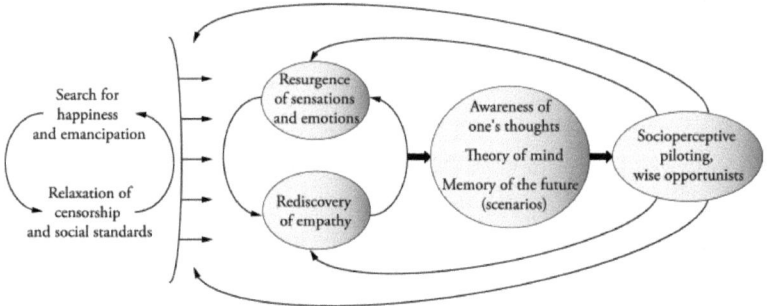

In a historical context where people are driven by a dominant search for happiness and emancipation, and in which rules and regulations are relaxed, there is a reawakening of sensations and emotions and a renewal of empathy which are mutually reinforcing. Their joint arousal develops awareness of the way one's inner life works, nourishing theories about mind and spirit and enriching perception of memories and the range of scenarios for available futures.

As a result, people improve their skills as socio-perceptive, opportunistic, and knowledgeable pilots of their lives.

They continue the learning process of navigating life and, in so doing, become more and more in touch with their sensations, emotions, and empathies.

The result is a rising level of emancipation and happiness in society, and continued deconstruction of outworn censorships and norms.

A NEW LIVING SOCIAL FABRIC

By the mid-1970s, it became clear to observers of socio-cultural change that transformation of personalities, or of ways of using one's intelligence, interacts with a transformation of the social fabric and the functioning of society. It was observed that people in the process of metamorphosis felt uncomfortable in a society that was still massive, hierarchical, segmented and enclosed. Unlike the students in May 1968, noiselessly, on tiptoe, those people abandoned the traditional society. In doing so, they devitalized society: conventions, taboos, rites, authorities, formal families, hierarchical enterprises, social classes, churches, political parties, etc., were all undermined.

The formerly rigid society became more permissive. It was increasingly easy not to respect the rules and to escape from social structures.

These people divorcing from the massive pyramidal society, with its top-down command and control mentality, did not shut themselves away in solitude. Humans are social animals, and it would be unbearable for them to do without connections, affection and love. The relatively autonomous and open-minded people we interviewed stood out from certain individuals around them and from some of the traditional, political, economic and cultural communities to which they were linked and with whom they no longer felt affinity. But they preserved their other connections and explored new ones. This took place in the 1970s and 1980s, shaping a radically new social fabric.

Searching for "little happinesses"

Seeking well-being, emotional support, and meaning, avoiding stress, painful constraints and clashes, people taking part in the transformation process connect and disconnect, reinforce or weaken connections according

to the positive and negative vibrations they perceive. To make a life that suits them, thousands and millions of Europeans and Americans choose independently to connect, disconnect or reconnect with people and groups that suit them and which accept or reject them

Decline of hierarchy

People leaving this old society were escaping from hierarchy. In social life and in the new collectives, rather than copying hierarchical behavior people turned to the imitation of equals: one models oneself more willingly on friends or those one admires, than on people who consider themselves superior.

Society started to become horizontal and heterarchical: clear and stable hierarchical scales and positions disintegrated and tended to be replaced by diverse and temporary influences that emerged and faded away according to circumstances. Leadership flowed from one to another. And within old organizations, the strength of hierarchical influence declined rapidly, making traditional and official positions difficult to maintain.

Towards autonomy and interpersonal exchanges

New social configurations were emerging from those billions of connections and changes in interrelations functioning as social systems. A multitude of collectivities are reinforced, weakened or transformed: couples form or dissolve; formal families restructure themselves into informality; personal networks of friends and professional networks emerge; waves or halos of emotion temporarily unite small groups or the whole earth; networks connect to other networks forming networks of networks; affinities discovered on the net permanently bring together people who, without knowing each other, feel close to each other; movements bring together those willing to undertake a common action while delinquent men and women retreat into isolation or ghettos.

Socio-cultural change and the development of electronic information and communication technologies are today stimulating and influencing each other.

Coupling with new information technologies

In the 1970s, new information and communication technologies were massive and hierarchical.

The development of techniques of interpersonal micro-telecommunication was encouraged by socio-cultural evolution and accelerated it markedly. From the mid-1980s onward, socio-cultural change and technological innovation in the fields of information and communication have become interdependent and in close synergy.

People hungry for autonomy and connections need to connect and disconnect freely and easily. The new society, in order to self-organize and self-regulate, developed new micro-telecommunication facilities (microcomputers first, followed by interconnection of personal computers, then Internet and, of course, mobile phones). These new tools, as they came together, created a positive feedback system that greatly accelerated the transformation of people and their society. This process continues to self-reinforce to the present day, with, for example, the proliferation of social networks and increasingly interactive applications for computers, smartphones, and tablets.

As early as 1977, the first personal computers intended for a large audience could be used by people who did not have a thorough knowledge of programming techniques. This was the beginning of a real revolution: in 1977 48,000 personal computers were sold worldwide; in 2001, this figure rose to 125 million, and in 2011 to 352 million. Unlike its predecessors, the personal and communicating microcomputer strengthened the autonomy of each person and extended the reach of networks by short-circuiting the center. The extremely rapid development of the microcomputer filled voids arising in two different fields: corporate executive demand and computer specialists' ambitions.

In many companies, executives who became more autonomous needed to escape the supervision typical of large organizations and act to on their own. This freedom was in opposition to the standard administrative management model of the 1980s, where information technology was embodied primarily in large centers managed by specialized services. Against the advice of management, information services, and even IBM - the leader in the field - executives and employees got to have personal microcomputers which made them able to search and process the information they needed on their own.

At the same time, executives began to feel the weight of administrative regulations hindered communication among departments. They arranged for their microcomputers to communicate directly with each other. Informal channels were thus formed, allowing executives to communicate on their own initiative, giving rise to informal networks which were faster and more efficient than the administrative circuits. During the 1980s, Cofremca was able to observe companies where such revolutions began spontaneously long before ratification by management.

In the mid-1980s, the use of microcomputers and their interconnection were seized on and imposed by executives eager for autonomy and departmental freedom. Once installed, networked microcomputers strengthened the demand for emancipation and unrestricted connection, dramatically accelerating the development of networks and sociosystems, and increasing the day-to-day influence of ordinary people.

The development of Internet technologies in the late 1960s was also inspired by the emancipation of specialized circles that had devised a fundamentally non-hierarchical network structure. We know that the Internet was initially a creation of the American military soldiers who were expected to live in a hierarchical culture. The researchers behind this discovery were in fact part of the Defense Advanced Research Projects Agency (DARPA), but they were soldiers of a particular kind, largely influenced by the hippie philosophy that was booming at the time[22]. It was the combination of peer-to-peer exchanges with the creation of the first search engines (making it possible to sort through data) that gave rise to the immense success of the Internet. Very quickly, it was perceived by the young researchers at MIT as a great opportunity for freedom: the possibility of peer-to-peer exchanges made it possible to short-circuit the established hierarchy[23].

---

22. Dominique Cardon, *Internet Democracy: Promises and Limits*, Threshold, 2010.
23. A French mathematician and electronics engineer, Louis Pouzin, was one of the leading designers of the Internet, but when France developed its Minitel, it preferred to administer it through the Ministry of Posts and Telegraphs, which straightway established a fundamentally hierarchic system unsuited to the metamorphosis in progress.

With some delay in relation to business organizations, the microcomputer, and very quickly the Internet, became present in everyone's home. In 1984 Apple launched Macintosh. In 1990, Windows began to be talked about, and soon dominated the market. To enter 50 million homes the radio took 37 years, television 13 years, and Internet only 5 years.

The new society of ordinary people

Over the past four decades, socio-cultural change has confirmed and accentuated the new directions taken during the "Glorious Thirties".

Instead of being anchored in rational thought, people are becoming increasingly connected to their vital forces and more and more autonomous as the old, massive, formal and hierarchical social fabric begins to disintegrate, and a new socio-culture emerges in which people see themselves as organic rather than organized.

From 1980 to the present day in Europe and North America, powerful processes have maintained and accelerated the socio-cultural metamorphosis that began after the war.

People continue to explore their animality and make new discoveries that fuel their autonomy and vitality. This motivates new behaviors, contributing to the self-organization and self-regulation of an increasingly complex and intensely alive organic social fabric, providing new areas for expressing one's personality.

Parents are evolving and doing things differently with their children, who in turn develop basic personality differences from the previous generation and who, perhaps, will raise their own children in a different way yet. Leaders and innovators are increasingly aware of the directions of changes under way, and produce innovations that respond to these changes, finding positive reactions in society and strengthening this movement.

Agents of change identify blockages or pathologies as they form, and try to intervene. These interwoven processes are leading to an astonishing society of non-hierarchized people, full of vitality, able to heal its wounds and organize its well-being. If it succeeds in blooming, this society will be the foundation for a future full of meaning for the human species.

Since the end of the twentieth century, a large number of new collectivities with complex structures has emerged from meetings and collaborations among ordinary people, networks, companies, authorities, and various other organizations. There are new examples every day. These structures are extremely diverse, may be ephemeral or lasting; some have no formal existence. Their borders can be blurry. Some are probably just trial runs in search of future solutions. These are new species of hybrid collectives in the process of emergence. Their typology has not yet been decided. This is the beginning of a self-organized society where many people take initiatives and catalyze innovations, and where many collectives, companies, associations, intermediaries, and other bodies bring together new hybrid solutions, many of which probably foreshadow some elements of the new approach to society-as-a-brain.

Part II. The socio-cultural metamorphoses of Homo Sapiens

SOCIETY-AS-A-BRAIN

Paths are emerging which could allow society to enter a new stage of its metamorphosis. A new leap in complexity would multiply empathic and non-hierarchical communications between ordinary people, the new collectives that are emerging, and effective actors from earlier society. This self-therapeutic society would be governed by its internal dynamics and its collective intelligence.

We do not know what forms this societal democracy and economy will take in a few decades, if metamorphosis continues. They will result from daily experiences and interactions. We know there will not be a pyramidal structure, that power will not be permanently concentrated in a definite body, but rather that it will be diffuse, emanating from the interplay of interactions. The organs that held power and influence in the hierarchical world will remain and survive only insofar as they have been able to communicate intimately with the society of people and its collectivities.

This society will be infinitely more complex than the hierarchical and rigidified societies invented by most civilizations since Sumer. Its organization might resemble that of our brain, where each neuron is connected to a very large number of others by a multitude of synapses.

These connections form groups at different levels. Several billion neurons and millions of billions of synaptic contacts "are organized into microcircuits, the combinations of which gradually form larger circuits, which in turn constitute networks and systems[24]". And we are beginning to understand that the system is even more

---
24. Antonio Damasio, *Self comes to mind: constructing the conscious brain*, Odile Jacob, 2010, p.26. This sentence of Damasio concerns the brain but also describes the metamorphosed society.

complex than we thought: recent research emphasizes the vital role of the glia. The brain contains almost one and a half times more glial cells than neurons; the two are in intense dialogue. Some of these glial cells integrate the messages brought from the environment by neurons and create the necessary adaptations and behaviors[25].

We can look at this metamorphosed society-as-a-brain on two levels. Hundreds of millions of people, like neurons, would connect to each other and to systems on different levels emanating from their interactions: families, friends, colleagues, social networks, companies, countries. From their interactions emerge on a second level - as the cerebral glia - regulations, shaping trends and bifurcations, which we will discuss again in the chapter on Artificial Intelligence. Connections that are used extensively reinforce each other. Others fade away. Networks and sets of networks are formed, evolve or stabilize without being definitively fixed. In this society, power is diffused and emerges from the interactions between the people and the systems that participate in its life. Like our brain, this society is not fully programmed. It learns and changes spontaneously and interacts with the world. Like our brain, it is not directed by a higher authority, such as a state, but by the interplay of its internal interactions and exchanges with its environments. It does not have a permanent controller. The orientations it adopts emanate from all the interactions between its organs and systems, one of them possibly finding itself, at a certain moment, in a position to show the way. Take the example of family life where leadership can move between the father, the mother and even the children according to the subject, or the life of a company where specialists take organizational

---

25. Yves Agid and Pierre Magistretti, *L'Homme glial : une révolution dans les sciences du cerveau*, Paris, Odile Jacob, 2018.

responsibilities as required by events. This society-as-a-brain is discussed in later chapters under the theme "living economy and societal democracy": a society of information and shared visions, networks, collaborations, societal coagulations. We cannot fully describe it yet, but advances in the neurosciences may bring us a model related to this evolving spirit of humanity and its ways of adapting and reacting.

Chapter 5.
The rise of spirituality

As we have said, the human mind or spirit creates cultures. The spirit, regulator of the Living, modeled by the body, is enriched by feelings, says Damasio, while conscience is born from the emotions. Here we are at the heart of human questioning about life and its links with death. Dating from the cave paintings we have living witness of this particularity of *Homo Sapiens* who, in addition to being a sociocultural animal, is also a spiritual animal.

HOMO SAPIENS, SPIRITUAL ANIMAL

Describing Homo Sapiens as a social animal we have already referred to primitive religion and the role of shamans. But as we have seen, since the Renaissance in Europe pride of place has been given to rationality.

Spiritual intelligence woke up during the nineteenth century, along with emotional-relational intelligence and focused consideration of sensory perception. As part of the metamorphosis, a new spirituality is being sought that seems to focus on human fulfillment and the relationship between Man and Nature, rather than fixed religious structures and a God or gods.

The European civilization from which we come believed in one all-powerful God who created the world and Man.

Since the eighteenth century and the Enlightenment, our civilization has slowly, painstakingly, destroyed this belief and dramatically reduced the influence of traditional religions.

This development was centered on reason, separated from theology and doctrine. This gave rise to contempt for superstitions, clairvoyance, astrology, and "folk remedies", but did not completely evacuate them from the daily lives of ordinary people or even leaders.

In the twentieth century rational intelligence began to take an interest in hidden dimensions. We sought to understand the variety of spiritual or religious practices and myths invented by humanity. Our civilization is undoubtedly the first to have undertaken this exploration in all directions.

We understand that Homo Sapiens - whether Paleolithic hunter-gatherer, Chinese peasant or Swedish employee - tends to believe in the coexistence of two worlds: the tangible world and the invisible world and to believe that these two worlds communicate, that the invisible influences the visible, and that humans (with the support of shamans, magicians, oracles, priests and other seers) can intervene in their relationship.

In the twentieth century, the transformation of the personality of Europeans and Americans has reinforced their interest in the invisible, but the rational mind remains on the lookout. People are reexamining the problem and are in the process of rebuilding their relationship with the invisible. Rational but open to the irrational in all its dimensions, they are interested in death, birth, life after death, reincarnations and hidden relationships between humans, and between Man and Nature. This analysis is usually personal, each working in his own way, carefully, maintaining a critical distance and without blindly believing.

A forerunner of this spiritual awakening, a sense of spiritual "simmering" marked the last decades of the nineteenth century with an interest in spiritism as an attempt to establish contact between the visible world and the invisible, while astrology - which fell asleep after its separation from astronomy at the end of the eighteenth century – also began to reemerge.

Europe, under the discipline of Newtonian science since the seventeenth century, began to undertake the exploration of Eastern wisdoms. The Theosophical Society, founded in 1875, promoted a form of syncretism (incorporating many Buddhist and Hindu precepts) which, according to the theosophists, is based on truths common to all religions: the Primordial Tradition.

It aspired to form the nucleus of the Universal Brotherhood of Humanity, to stimulate the comparative study of religions, philosophies and sciences and to study the unexplained laws of nature and the latent powers of man.

The attraction of Eastern spirituality

Throughout the twentieth century, a growing proportion of our Western contemporaries were interested in approaches to spirituality born in other civilizations. Oriental wisdoms, notably Buddhist, Taoist, and Hindu, occupy a great place in contemporary neo-spiritualist syncretism. Belief in reincarnation is spreading throughout the West. Buddhist monasteries and Zen centers are successfully establishing themselves in Europe and America. We borrow their concepts, their rituals and their physical and mental exercises to bring about spiritual awakening. We practice meditation, yoga, and martial arts. More than one in ten French people say they feel close to Buddhism.

There are profound affinities between Buddhism and the sensibilities that are emerging in the West. For example, the Buddhist approach - non-dogmatic, non-authoritarian, individualistic, ecumenical, tolerant - which requires less observance and more working on oneself, is in tune with the psychological and spiritual attitudes of a society marked by growing autonomy, empathy and maturation of personalities. Buddhism is the antithesis of the culture of suffering, sacrifice and sin from which we are detaching ourselves. Karma, the law of consequences and the interdependence of phenomena, meets our increasing openness to complexity and our intuitive understanding of reality as interwoven systems and processes. The interdependence of things and beings is consistent with our ecological conception of reality and the notion of ecosystems. With the notion of immanence, the idea that life emanates from itself, that the process feeds the process, we find that the Buddhist tradition meets our own discoveries. The quest for serenity and harmony, central to Buddhists, is among the dominant concerns of stressed Westerners.

This meeting does not mean that tens of millions of Westerners are converting to Buddhism, but rather that an awareness of its texts, its rites and its practices helps people in the West find new ways to lead their lives. Buddhist influence permeates a large number of syncretic propositions centered on personal development.

The Chinese ancestral wisdom of Tao (or Dao) is also in resonance with the evolution of our perception of nature and action, and seduces many leaders of American and European companies. The principle of "non-action" rules out forced, voluntarist action. It suggests not inaction but slackening the reins, an accompanying action that follows the folds and natural currents of the terrain.

The resurgence of a humanist Christianity

Christianity's emphasis on sin, penance and suffering runs counter to a hedonistic culture of fulfillment. The Catholic Church's rejection of birth control shocks populations concerned with ecological balance. Its hierarchical and authoritarian structure, as well as its misogyny, are driving away populations more and more centered on autonomy and feminism.

The New Age wave did little for the traditional Catholic and Protestant churches in Europe and North America - except for some evangelical churches that feed on the collective emotion of the participants. But it is possible that Christian churches could find themselves in agreement with metamorphosis, as they become more peaceful, ecumenical, even syncretic. Many of their followers make up their own combination of personal beliefs that may contradict some of those in their church and borrow others from other religions or philosophies. They also choose the rites they practice. A fairly widespread charismatic impulse and new rites often invented by the base provide a collective emotional warmth and sometimes a sense of awakening that can answer a deficit of emotion and open the way to moments of spiritual communion.

After Vatican II and May 1968, new forms of individual or collective Christian spirituality appeared in the West or were reinforced. In search of their identity and seeking deeper meaning in their lives, many Christians consciously explored an approach to spirituality that suited them by rejecting the institutional side of their church. They went in search of places of silence and spiritual healing, centers they found both in the West and in the East: Franciscan movements, charismatic movements, institutes of human development as in Quebec, spiritual summer schools. This emergent spirituality is the response to a demand from the laity rather than the clergy, mingling forms of Eastern spirituality, Orthodox chants, Christian Ashrams in India, Christian retreats in Buddhist, Hindu or Zen seminaries. Emotion is at the center of all this research rather than intellectual thought: the Dalai Lama has called on young people to create a happier century and said: "the world might be better without religions". He has said that he could be "the last Dalai Lama". Behind all these approaches lies a humanistic and spiritual search for a peaceful, fraternal world that echoes this era's quest for meaning.

By his attitudes and his communication Pope Francis is reducing the institutional and hierarchical aspect of the Roman Church. He focuses on the Gospels, the human person, empathy, compassion. On questions of universal morality, he avoids categorical condemnation ("Who am I to judge?"), and seems ready to let local developments occur. He is moving in the direction of a society of people.

In doing so, he is arousing favorable reactions among Western populations, even unbelievers. It is significant that the new pope chose the name of Francis, *il poverello*, the friend of the poor, but also the friend of nature, the one who reconciled Man and Nature as parts of Creation, the author of the Cantico del Sole. The encyclical *Laudato Si* is a hymn to our planet, "our shared home".

New experiences of spirituality

Humans whose sensoriality develops and whose personality is transformed discover the essence or new aspects of spirituality.

Many enter more or less deliberately into a deep exploration-evaluation of their inner life. This is a very different exploration from the examination of conscience or the moral, rational or strategic self-criticism that characterized internal dialogue during the preceding sociocultural period. Their reason works on their experiences. They discover themselves bigger, deeper, more multiple than they thought. They realize that they have sleeping potentials that have woken up. They often have the intuition that the human species has great potential for fulfillment.

On their own and together, they discover that they may, in some cases, find themselves in a particular state of consciousness or sensation that is enjoyable, in which they feel more peaceful, more empathetic, more fulfilled, and which gives them the feeling of better understanding the meaning of their life and the way forward.

Some become aware of the circumstances, settings, and types of meetings likely to feed this meditative state, and seek them in various spiritual environments. This movement favors the development of allegiances and practices centered on experiences rather than on beliefs, texts and dogmas.

Many of these people feel themselves close to animals - especially mammals - and yet much superior to them. They are more or less aware that it is their minds and brains that make the difference. They wonder not only about themselves but about the humanity as a whole.

The result is a proliferation of new assumptions, beliefs and attempts at self-transformation mixed up with fundamental questions: Who are we? Where do we come from? Where are we going? What is our place in nature? What could be the meaning of our life?

Neuroscience, spirituality, unconscious

Certain advances in neuroscience intersect with people's deeper concerns. For example, in the 1970s, many Europeans and Americans, informed by the press and television of the discoveries of Roger Sperry and Michael Gazzaniga concerning the specialization of the two cerebral hemispheres, felt too dominated by their left brain (reputed rational and logical), and embarked on exercises to develop their right brain.

Similarly, the discovery of mirror neurons by Giacomo Rizzolatti and his team in the early 1990s struck many minds. It helped people to better understand the bodily and active, non-intellectual character of empathy and collective intelligence. It fueled their belief that mind and matter, psychology and biology were two sides of the same reality.

Spectacular advances in neuroscience are stimulating the reflections of a relatively large audience and influencing the dominant representations of the brain. Researchers' attention is shifting from the cortex and artificial intelligence, to the living and total brain (including its limbic and reptilian parts and the brain stem, i.e., the entire central nervous system).

Their shared message is that the human brain is extremely adaptable, that it is potentially more than a machine for thinking, but also for surviving, for improving life conditions, and for connecting with others and with life. Free Will and Reason - of which we had been so proud - are put back in their places. For example, they show that often our brain decides before we have consciously taken a decision, in fact that we cannot rely on reason alone (without either emotion or intuition) to lead us to act suitably within the complexity of Living.

This change of focus was expected, and easy to understand, among men and women who have already advanced in the integration of their reason, emotions, and spirit. It encourages them to push their personal development even further.

Research is developing on some of the mysterious dimensions of life in society, arts, management; this could be a prelude to a paradigm shift. There are similar bodies of research: on near-death experiences; at the Mind and Life Institute, born from the collaboration between the XIVth Dalai Lama and the Chilean neuroscientist Francisco Varela, which explores the relationship between science and Buddhism; in the United States (Princeton, Berkeley, University of Madison-Wisconsin) and Germany (Max Planck Institute of Leipzig), on the influence on the brain of long-term mind training.

Recent research suggests that some mysteries of life might be better understood if biology comes closer to quantum physics, according to which a particle can be in different places at the same time or can cross impassable barriers[26].

---

26. Jim Al-Khalili and Johnjoe McFadden, *Life on the Edge: The Coming of Age of Quantum Biology*, Bantam Press, 2014.

The search for meaning

The old beliefs and ideologies that gave meaning to life are outworn. A dogmatically defined God has no place in the daily life of a majority of Europeans, but during the 1970s and 1980s, the number of people in search of meaning increased greatly.

The major ideologies that had attracted people - nationalism, fascism, communism, modernity, progress - were now cold. Becoming more personal, expressive and socio-perceptive, they became aware that they were being manipulated by the consumer society, and the race for social standing and modernity. They were wearing themselves out to achieve goals that were ultimately insignificant. Bureaucratic work reduced them to pawns. Revolution and Class Struggle were in fact lures. The scientific and technical progress in which they had believed were sources of social perversity.

The phenomenon expanded rapidly, and from the beginning of the 1980s, observatories of socio-cultural change in the United States and France informed their clients that the quest for meaning had become a shaping trend in daily life.

On the ruins of values passed down from above and inherited from the past (Progress, Competition, Success), people rebuilt personal theories of meaning from their daily experience - seemingly the basis for a new system of values emerging from below. A new humanism of fulfillment, cooperation and optimization is thus taking the place of a modernity made of progress, competition, maximization and success. It is about bringing lasting fulfillment, harmony and vitality to oneself, to those we love, to our communities and, ultimately, to humanity.

One seeks to alleviate tensions and suffering, and to feel one's cooperation with those who act in this way. The combined exercise of rational, emotional-relational and spiritual intelligences seems to lead to wisdom.

This is a real break-away not only from the consumer-competition society, but more fundamentally from the previous stage of European civilization, which was centered on competition and maximizing benefits: feudal competition, among courtiers; between aristocrats and bourgeois; among bourgeois; among consumers; between parties of right and left; among nations; and among struggling classes. Competition and maximization give way to optimization.

SOCIETAL DEBATE INCLUDES THE UNCONSCIOUS

Beginning in the 1920s, the brain, the psyche and society have been subjects for discussion among those who are trying to expand their understanding of themselves in nature, and to find ways of developing human potential.

Psychanalysts - Freud, Jung and others - drew our attention to the major role of the unconscious, myths and hidden pressures. Jung stimulated consideration of the collective unconscious, archetypes, synchronicity, and opened the way to examination of the hidden dimensions of human experience. The means of communication of these subjects promoted their theories. We examined our dreams, our complexes, and our unconscious, as well as those of our entourage. In short, we explored the manner in which we bathe in the human collectivity and in nature.

Georges Gurdjieff was a particularly notable initiator of such subjects. In 1922, he opened his Priory Institute at Avon, near Paris, and then in New York. His teaching and the exercises he employed consisted mainly in assisting the spiritually "asleep" or "mechanized" to wake up, by bringing their intellect (brain), emotions (heart) and body (belly) into better balance. Numerous Gurdjieff groups were established after his death in 1949.

LEARNING TO DIALOGUE WITH ONE'S BRAIN: TAKE BREAKS

Beginning in the 1930s, Alfred Korzybski and his General Semantics Institute, based on the neurological knowledge of the period, encouraged millions of Americans and thousands of Europeans to establish a dialogue with their own brains, practicing "cortico-thalamic pauses to control their emotions" and remembering that "the map is not the territory"[27].

General semantics aimed to move beyond the logic of Aristotelian thought (principles of identity, non-contradiction and the excluded middle) which, by keeping the West in a conflictual (either/or) logic, had, according to Korzybski, been one of the principal causes of the First World War. For Korzybski, the knowledge that men have of reality is limited by the structures of their nervous system and their language. They cannot experience the world directly, but only grasp it through verbal or non-verbal abstractions. In order to act wisely they need to learn to become aware of these mechanisms of abstraction.

---

27. Alfred Korzybski, Science and Sanity, An Introduction to Non-Aristotelian Systems and General Semantics, 1st edition, 1933. Manhood of Humanity, The Science and Art of Human Engineering, Institute of General Semantics, 1950

The aim of general semantics is to resolve human problems more effectively than hitherto, when the dominant logical structures were Aristotelian, Newtonian or Cartesian.

The spread of non-Aristotelian thinking should enable the development of more harmonious human relations and allow humanity to transition into its age of adulthood.

MYTHS OF THE FUTURE

The theory of evolution towards point Omega

This is without doubt the most successful myth produced during the course of the twentieth century. In it, Pierre Teilhard de Chardin (1881-1955) combined rationality and spirituality. A recognized scholar (geologist, paleontologist, theoretician of evolution) as well as a Jesuit priest profoundly attached to his faith, he sketched a history of the universe and life incorporating all the major knowledge of his period (Darwinian evolution, quantum mechanics, thermodynamics).

A leading paleontology researcher, he compared the newly discovered early hominids to other mammals and showed the increase in encephalic complexity characteristic of the first anthropoids. He emphasized the growing complexity of life leading to the emergence of the central nervous system as the vehicle for human intelligence and spirituality.

Parallel to this, he insisted on the humanization and moral evolution that resulted in mammals paying more attention to their young than reptiles, but with less solidarity between themselves than human beings.

He anticipated globalization and the development of communications systems, and proposed a theory of individual consciousnesses which, communicating more and more intensely between themselves, would form centers that together would form a film of thought enveloping the planet: the noosphere, preparing the "Omega point" and the coming of the "cosmic Christ".

This theory is once more arousing considerable interest. Today we see that globalization and the extremely rapid development of social networks and portable telephones have caused our societies to make a great leap forward in complexity, allowing for the development of a "noosphere". As regards the brain, a number of neuroscience researchers accept the idea that self-awareness emerges above a certain level of complexity. It is not unthinkable that once a superior level of complexity has been achieved, a collective human consciousness could emerge.

New Age

During the 1960s and 70s, a multitude of extremely diverse beliefs and practices from the East and West - sometimes originating from the dawn of time - were agglomerated under the label New Age[28].

It included traces of theosophy, Gurdjieff, Jung, astrology, Buddhism, Sufism, shamans, modern psychology, alternative medicine, and the peace and love ideology of the young people of the 1960s.

---

28. Marilyn Ferguson, *The Aquarian Conspiracy*, Jeremy P. Tarcher, 1980.

An ecological morality and neo-spirituality

The idea that the human species, all living beings and the planet Earth together form an ecosystem that is now dangerously unbalanced by recent developments in human activity, has made serious progress.

The concept gave rise in the 1970s to an ideology, and in some countries to political parties, which have failed to convince a majority of citizens or to profoundly change the behavior of our governments.

But in the 1990s and 2000s, a collective consciousness began to emerge: ordinary people are more and more numerous to feel that the human species inhabits nature like a fish in water, and to survive and develop must optimize its relationship with its surroundings.

These people find a deep meaning in banal behaviors that contribute to the environment: they turn off lights, save water, travel less for pleasure.

An ecology-conscious morality and neo-spirituality are emerging. They echo the Gaia theory, conceived by James Lovelock[29]. The planet Earth with its living and non-living elements constitutes a self-regulating ecosystem, a living organism which regulates its elements for the benefit of the whole system. This idea of Mother Earth as a living organism has been found in various ancient religions.

James Cameron's film, Avatar, which focuses on ecological neo-spiritualism, was a huge success. It brings us into the privacy of the inhabitants of the planet Pandora. The Na'Vi live in symbiosis with animal and vegetable nature and their bio-spiritual vitality terminates, for the pleasure

---

29. James Lovelock, *The Ages of Gaia: A Biography of Our Living Earth*, Norton, 1988.

of the spectators, in triumphing over the rational, warlike, mechanical and industrial logic of American capitalism.

The rise of personal development

At the end of the Second World War, humanistic psychologists or psychotherapists such as Abraham Maslow, Carl Rogers or Fritz Perls offered perspectives of development and fulfillment for human beings. In their wake, many seminars, working groups or chapels proliferated in Europe and North America.

Personal development is a theme common to most of the approaches we have just mentioned, but it is also a business sector in itself and a market that has taken on considerable importance in recent decades.

The belief has spread that humans tend to fall asleep and that they could wake up; that their brains have inactive potentials that they could actualize; that their education and their past lives have fixed them in attitudes that would be out of kilter in a new world and which they could try to get rid of.

Growing up and fulfilling oneself and optimizing the ecosystems in which one participates tend to become meaningful individual and collective goals. Many companies and organizations are involved in this movement.

Today, in Europe and America, there are growing numbers of networks, circles and seminars designed to help their participants to make better use of their brains in their personal and professional lives. There are training courses focused on personal development, the discovery of new dimensions of the mind, collective intelligence, anticipation, socio-perception, social skills. We discover, for example, how to conduct one's life wisely or how to be a leader in a society that has abandoned its former models and no longer functions on the basis of authority or hierarchy. Even in France these seminars are becoming an accepted phenomenon, and are less frequently qualified as sectarian by the advocates of a rigid rationalism.

Seminars focused on Mindfulness are very successful. They are inspired by Buddhist practices.

A CENTURY OF THE MIND AND OF THE SPIRIT

Humanity has known certain periods of spiritual growth. The fifth century BC was one such - within a limited period extending to perhaps two centuries the world saw the arrival of the Buddha, Lao Tzu, Confucius, the major Biblical prophets and the Greek philosophers. Today we are living through a new century of the spirit, in which we are aware of transferring from a narrowly rational vision of a fragmentary world to a perception of the complexity of interconnected life encompassing the entire planet. Can this growth in awareness lead to a period of deeper reflection, a century of spiritual growth enabling humanity to evolve further? Where have we got to?

The humanist psycho-bio-spiritualism that is developing in Europe and North America is so diverse that it may seem incoherent. It develops discreetly, without centralizing organizations, without established leaders reigning over large groups. Its representatives emerge here and there, as with all the hybrid collectives whose proliferation we will observe in the following chapters. This movement seems weak and tenuous when compared to the great religions of humanity. But, unlike those monotheisms, it is tolerant and syncretic. And it has a profound underlying unity: it focuses on the development of potentials and the optimization of people and humanity within their ecosystems. It unites much more than it divides or challenges, and is thus a seedbed for major evolutionary possibilities.

Some feel the probable existence of a dimension of reality with the dead, man with nature, the present with the future. They have the intuition that, based on advances in scientific research in the twenty-first century, humanity may be able to enter a new, more harmonious era of its development, that cultural evolution is pushing us in that direction, but that we need to help this evolution to come about.

Cultural metamorphosis: Man and the cosmos
Getting closer to nature

From biblical Old Testament man as master or guardian of nature, our century is returning to a cosmological dimension of humanity immersed in nature. This is felt today in the development of ecological awareness, especially in children. This movement has gone global and is expressed in a wide variety of ways: as a return to the land, a focus on cultures linked to nature (for example the awakening interest in the Kogis Indians[30], even among some Western companies), the focus on Asian spiritualities, etc.

---

30. Eric Julien, *Le chemin des 9 mondes - les Indiens Kogis peuvent nous enseigner les mystères de la vie* (The way of the 9 worlds - the Kogis Indians can teach us the mysteries of life) Paris, Albin-Michel, 2001.

Man's artistic developments

Throughout the history of mankind, great artistic masterpieces have been the expression of spirituality in Homo Sapiens, from the cave at Chauvet and prehistoric shrines, through the era of developing civilizations up until today. Art has been the expression of socio-cultural metamorphoses. Beginning with the Renaissance - the first European metamorphosis - artistic expression was essentially centered on representing humanity. By the end of the nineteenth century, going beyond realism and "photographic" representation, by allowing primary colors and sounds to burst into expressions of sensations and emotions, a pictorial, musical, and sculptural artistic metamorphosis has prefigured a societal transformation. Impressionist painters and composers aimed for the essence of things, following a path expressed by Kandinsky as "spirituality in art": color and line are the artistic expression of the deepest sensations of the artist and evolving society in which he lives. Picasso, Miro and many others were able to denounce the horrors of their troubled times and war, and also to move forward through another viewpoint, like that of Nicolas de Staël, on the path of metamorphosing life, of links with the earth, with the cosmos, with the poetic, musical transcription of their emotions.

The search for the human element in all its dimensions remains central. Today, the vibrations of the sun and stars are transcribed musically in "Galactic" concerts, expressions of a spiritual search.

The emotions raised all over the world by the fire at the cathedral of Notre-Dame de Paris are signs of the spiritual consciousness shared among believers and non-believers alike.

Walking, the quest for meaning in life

The development of "walkers", pilgrims seeking humanity on mountain paths, along the seashore, on the road to Compostela, on Japanese islands, "providential" encounters, synchronicity, convergences in "mythical places" - the temple of Karnak, the ruins of

Part II. The socio-cultural metamorphoses of Homo Sapiens

> Angkor, Mont St. Michel, Hindu ashrams: these are all forms of expression in the century of Meaning.

In his book, "Knowledge, Ignorance, Mystery", Edgar Morin[31] dares to put question marks around the place of man in the universe: "I live more and more with the awareness and feeling of the presence of the unknown in the known…"

This neo-spiritualism is perhaps one of the dimensions of metamorphosis. It is emerging from the intersection of the collapse of earlier vehicles of meaning, and the acceptance of complexity by the rational mind. A source of meaning, it is one of the main fuels for the proliferation of new collectivities cropping up in the society of ordinary people.

All socio-cultures, all civilizations have felt the need to tell stories, to invent myths that make sense of their existence. Our own socio-culture very evidently works in this way. But we have not succeeded yet. Humanity's non-Aristotelian adulthood announced by Korzybski, the New Age's Age of Aquarius, or Teilhard de Chardin's Omega point, where a happy and peaceful society will allow everyone to find their own place while still participating with others in collective construction, are the dreams of many. We need a driving myth, a story or stories that would provide answers to our fundamental questions, in tune with our dominant intuitions, sufficiently consistent with the advances of scientific research, and acceptable to our rational intelligence.

---

31. Paris, Fayard, 2017.

Perhaps we must wait for new discoveries in biology and neuroscience, which will fuel the myth-building process that can consolidate metamorphosis.

In this century, Homo Sapiens is making a leap forward in the evolution of life: from one animal among others, he became hunter gatherer, inventive, spiritual, artistic, then a farmer-breeder villager, occupying the planet, expanding its population, inventing civilizations, writing, the State, religions. Sapiens is now going through a new phase, that of the humanist metamorphosis, the blossoming of man.

Spiritual intelligence is growing stronger and reorganizing itself, dialoguing with other forms of intelligence. New spiritualities are developing, earlier forms of spirituality are transforming and combining: Pope Francis and the Dalai Lama are symbols of this. The prodigious development in the West of techniques of meditation, prayer, and personal development, are enabling Homo Sapiens to become a wiser species, better able to govern itself in complexity.

We are at a major crossroad: Which way will we go? Towards growth, or an aborted metamorphosis?

HAPPYMORPHOSE

Part III
A great bifurcation: hesitations in humanist metamorphosis

If human evolution continues with the same orientations, a relatively harmonious, balanced and flourishing society of people will undoubtedly prove sufficiently informed to meet the geopolitical, ecological and biological challenges that Homo Sapiens will face in the twenty-first century.

It is tempting to attribute this new development to living intelligence, that is, to the biosphere's capacity to sustain life, to reproduce it and to develop it. We know, however, from Ilya Prigogine, that while dissipative systems evolve according to very stable shaping trends, they are nonetheless subject to bifurcations. The humanist metamorphosis could deviate in an authoritarian or a chaotic direction, even if it were to re-emerge a few centuries later.

Three threats weigh on this metamorphosis:

- the resistance of large financialized companies,
- uncertainties related to the extremely rapid expansion of digital technology,
- and the persistence of democracy as we practice it.

Let's take a closer look at the field.

Chapter 6.
Towards a living societal economy

At the end of the twentieth century, a large number of new collectivities with complex forms emerged from meetings and collaborations among ordinary people, networks, companies, powers and various organizations. There are new ones every day. Their forms and status are extremely diverse. These are new species of hybrid collectivities in the process of emergence.

Intense interpersonal relationships between autonomous and affective people, more concerned with optimization than competition, skillfully managing their close relationships, are experienced as carriers of well-being and fulfillment.

Many ordinary people have an explicit citizen ambition. They seek to intervene actively and deliberately in society to mend its pathologies and optimize its operation. While being very focused on their personal development, their micro-socio-systems and their own way of life, these "social therapists" are driven by a visceral urge to take care of people, repair damage in their society and enrich its vitality. This commitment gives meaning to their lives by involving them in building an intensely vibrant society and socio-economy.

The discomfort of many actors in the old hierarchical and bureaucratic society is the driving force behind the development of hybrid collectivities. Capitalist business leaders, mayors, local or national politicians are becoming aware of their inadequacy as regards changing society and the economy.

Top-down command and control works badly, the power of the state crumbles, bureaucratic procedures lead to rejections and blockages, consumers are not participants, breakthrough innovations threaten to destabilize markets.

Many realize more or less clearly that in order to succeed in this or that type of transformation, they must interact with other players, sometimes to cooperate with individuals, sometimes with collectivities arising from the society of people, with whom to discover new ways to operate.

THE NEW CREATURES: HYBRID COLLECTIVITIES

"Le vivant se bricole"[32]: Living is a patchwork

Between complicit observers we call them "new animals" or "new creatures". They take extremely varied forms.

Sometimes they are isolated people who connect with others - for example within their business, their city, or the school where their children go to school - with the idea of opening the dialogue. The link between them sometimes remains informal, even secret, or stabilizes in the form of a declared association, or even an enterprise. Sometimes well-established associations join other collectivities,

---

32. François Jacob, *La logique du vivant : une histoire de l'hérédité*, op. cit.

several companies in the region, or even representatives of the public authorities, to initiate cooperation.

These are informal networks, declared associations, sustainable cooperatives, *ad hoc* collaborations, ecosystems, for-profit and not-for-profit businesses, public agencies, think tanks, clubs, foundations, etc.

Living socio-culture experiments: companies taking new forms, start-ups, social businesses...

Start-ups have sprung up over the last two decades, often in garages, exploring the possibilities of new information technologies. The *mores* and rules of the dominant economic paradigms have facilitated neither their birth nor their development. Some have been strangled by finance. Others survived. Some have remained small and take full advantage of networking. Some are extremely successful, such as Google. Together, they have transformed our lives and those of businesses.

They are dealing with a market in which they must find profitability, but at the same time their success depends very much on their fine adjustment to society as it develops. They thus have a foot in both camps, in the commercial economy and the societal economy; they are expected to contribute to the common good.

We have seen their development first in California, then across the United States, then in Europe, with social entrepreneurs launching at the local, national or global levels, developing social businesses, a new type of hybrid organization that explicitly combines two perspectives deemed contradictory: the "not-for-profit" and the "for-profit" operations. They primarily fulfill a social mission rather than seeking profits. But unlike most charities, these organizations generate their own sustainable incomes and are not based on philanthropy. Revenues are held and reinvested rather than distributed to shareholders. These new companies, like thousands of Silicon Valley startups before them, sometimes start on the initiative of small groups of intensely motivated people. Others, like Danone Ecosystem, emanate from large international groups in search of the new socio-economy. Examples of hybrid social entrepreneurship bloom everywhere: for example, Ardelaine, in the gorges of France's Ardeche department, with the reconstruction of an abandoned village, through development of activities, creation of a weaving factory, garment making, shared gardens. In this way life returns to weakened areas.

In 2015, the climate was for innovation. New startups launched in the United States, Sweden, France and elsewhere, exploring Big Data, cloud computing, Internet of things, biotechnology, robotics, 3D printers, biomimicry, stem cells, synthetic meat, new methods of teaching and education, online trade and exchange, disintermediation, collaborative platforms, nanotechnologies, artificial intelligence, energy transition, ecological transition.

A growing proportion of young men and women who graduate from business schools would like to avoid becoming employees in a large, conventional company. They dream of building a life that makes sense, a life whose direction can change along the way, or of finding the idea that would allow them to start their own start-up or a micro-enterprise that would work for the common good.

Social networks, blogs, tweets and buzz

Companies are becoming aware that they operate within a complex ecosystem with economic, social, societal and ecological aspects upon which they depend and which depend on them.

By rapidly multiplying the number of connections between people, sources of information and communication opportunities, by locating people and keeping in touch with each other as they move, the system and the complex society it irrigates have mutated.

We must remember the way in which, forty years ago, a network of self-organized and self-organizing networks began to emerge. People were becoming autonomous, and were uncomfortable in a hierarchical society, rigid and pre-organized in compartments and groups. They began to escape on tiptoe. But they did not leave aiming to be alone. Hungry for affective warmth and insertion, they connected here and there with kindred spirits and opportunities, starting the first networks of proximity. They also felt more or less connected to various collectivities, halos, *philae*, movements, extending the coverage and multiplying the meshes of these first networks.

The success of the Internet and enhancements of the portable telephone powerfully fed the movement in the late 1990s. Email, general more or less communal social networks, sites, blogs, tweets, forums, corporate networks, collaborative platforms, etc., all spread very quickly and took on board dozens and then hundreds of millions of Internet users. Social media were being set up, expanded or replaced: Yahoo, Friendster, BlackPlanet, LinkedIn, Amazon, Wikipedia, MySpace, Facebook, Google, Twitter, and many more. In some systems crowdsourcing or users (Wikipedia) participated in development. On the networks now frequented by hundreds of millions of Internet users in different languages but also in the form of images, information from all over the world circulates, discussions occur, patterns appear and waves of collective intelligence are formed. Some blogs attract attention and become influential. Mass media and institutional actors can analyze the buzz, amplify it, and interact with it.

Today, one or a few clicks, free of charge, day and night, everyone can connect to a neighbor in the apartment next door or a friend on the other side of the world, or discover a new email friend whose profile fits. Everyone can express oneself, hoping to find an audience, participate in a discussion on a topic of interest or a collective project, access missing information within minutes, be aware of books that have just come out. Everyone can participate in feeding our collective intelligence and consciousness.

The multiplication of these interconnections and networks in permanently self-organizing forms confers a remarkable capacity for innovation, flexibility and a very great reactivity for living society. This is not to overlook potential abuses of the system - manipulations and "fake news" - which we will discuss in the chapter on digital intelligence.

Think tanks and do tanks

These complex organizations are distinct from political parties, churches and representatives of particular economic interests (lobbies) because they emanate from the society of people or from the new socio-economy they seek to influence. They are associations, think tanks and do tanks, NGOs, laboratories, training centers, networks of consultants, etc.

The most typical currently operate from a therapeutic perspective: they want to help people or certain categories of people, certain communities, society or some of its sectors to suffer less, to heal, to blossom, to free themselves, to grow. They are fueling metamorphosis and are often initial drafts of pilot cells for the emerging society.

These societal transformation and regulation agencies are guided by empathy, an intuition of metamorphosis, a view of what makes sense, the feeling of a mission to be accomplished. Human rights, direct or participatory democracy, disintermediation, more humane businesses, birth control, ecology, feminism, transparency and anti-corruption, channeling the power of superpowers, personal development, and collective protest are among the themes that motivate them.

Together, even if they are not in contact, they contribute significantly to the concerted interactions that influence the evolution of socio-culture.

In addition to these powerful agencies and networks, ordinary people, staff, executives or managers in a company or administration often play a decisive role as agents of change in their organization. They are not ideologues but pragmatic humanists who suffer from being treated and seeing their colleagues treated as pawns. They are committed to their business and seek to make sense of their work. Socioperceptives, they are skillful and often find allies with whom they cooperate to make certain procedures evolve. Their role is considerable.

New collaborations

Sustainable egalitarian connections - among people, companies, associations, foundations, public agencies (especially local ones), and even governments - form a new whole, bring out latent synergies among the participants, and try to obtain results that would have been inaccessible to each of the members in isolation. In early 2010, we learned every week of the birth in Europe or North America of new intervention cooperatives with defined goals.

For example, political parties from opposite sides get closer and cooperate to form a coalition government, seeking to take a fresh look at the problems of today.

To take another example, under the impetus of the Clinton Climate Initiative, the largest cities in the world have formed a cooperative network to collaborate in reducing their carbon emissions, their use of fossil fuels and their pollution. Together they learn from the progress and failures of each participant. The largest ports on the planet have imitated them. Large global companies with affinities among them have come together to pursue similar goals.

Here, a hundred small and medium-sized enterprises operating in the region have joined forces to jointly make use of a small number of specialists and senior executives, none of whom are permanently needed by any particular company. Elsewhere, large, old-fashioned, slow-moving companies are focusing on collaboration with start-ups, forming networks to discover and initiate major paths of innovation.

Similarly, companies are committed to cooperate in developing management methods that are both human and effective. Others aim to improve their relationships with their subcontractors. Some form cooperative networks with local authorities and associations to find ways to reduce unemployment in their labor pool.

In the coming years, collaborating ensembles will flourish and exert a major transformative action that will enhance the vitality and resilience of participants as well as the production of common goods that people expect.

The intuition is spreading in various circles of the society of people that we are facing major changes, that we must prepare ourselves for a different future, but that many of our leaders are looking the wrong way. This awareness feeds the development of think tanks, discussion circles, innovation laboratories, networks for monitoring weak signals, forecasting. Together they are helping to create a climate conducive to innovation.

Artificial creations, artifacts that come to life

Smart innovators design an organization involving different stakeholders connected to each other digitally in such a way that the system comes to life, self-regulates and produces a powerful or improved service.

In recent years, many major cities in Europe have installed self-service bicycle systems. For the system to come to life without a hitch, the IT and human connections must be permanently available between the cyclists, their credit cards, the bicycles, the stations, the trucks which move the bicycles from one station to another according to need, and, of course, repair services. The various players, who are well informed in real time, react appropriately and the system becomes self-regulating.

Another example is smart grids for the production, distribution and consumption of electricity. A computer system connects the various sources of electricity production, distribution networks and users and consumers of all types in real time in order to reduce overall consumption, limit the use of the most polluting power stations, and integrate millions of renewable energy sources.

Instead of blindly consuming electricity whose quantity and cost only appear on the bill after the fact, the user has a smart meter that allows him to consume under the best conditions at the most suitable time.

Connection platforms similar to Uber, BlaBlaCar, and Airbnb are spreading rapidly.

METAMORPHOSIS FEEDS ON ITSELF

This profusion of new collectivities has begun to establish a new stage in the society of people, an extension of the driving forces underlying the humanist metamorphosis.

These collectivities are both products and promoters of the self-organization of a new society.

The vast majority stands at the same egalitarian level: in their networks, there are no stable leaders, influence circulates, and there is much discussion from which emerges collective intelligence. Adjusting to each other, without formalism or hierarchy, participants are involved in adjustments that are more biological than bureaucratic, more emotional than ideological. They influence participants in hierarchical organizations who can no longer contribute to the production of the common good unless they change their hierarchical attitude and collaborate on the same level as the society of people. The entanglements of these hybrid collectivities raise the level of complexity of society in general and make it increasingly ungovernable by hierarchy and bureaucracy. Their participants transform society. They de-centralize, de-bureaucratize, de-hierarchize, and de-ideologize it.

Through their actions, through the ecosystems and the self-regulating structures they organize, new collectivities participate in a multitude of functions of general interest. New collectivities can mend some of the organizational defects that are suffered by ordinary people (for example, by decreasing local unemployment, improving schooling in the area, helping to create energy savings, encouraging a coalition government to replace a partisan government, etc.).

Such new structures and the people involved are on the lookout for deficits in the common good, for signs of dangerous bifurcations, for opportunities to progress. Consciously or not, these structures and these people are promoting the current metamorphosis. Their growing numbers probably increase the chances that the metamorphosis will continue.

Commitment to their collectivities gives those involved the feeling of participating in the development and optimization of their society and of having their say. They find meaning and gratification. But this feeling is often ephemeral and fuels the realization that they have very few opportunities to really participate in the life of their company, city or country, which are often dominated by old power structures. This results in intense frustrations and calls for change.

A NEW ECONOMY OF SHARING AND COOPERATION

People with this sort of profile connect with other people with the same or complementary profiles or with goals that they share. An economy of personal initiative, collaboration and facilitation rather than domination and appropriation is gaining ground every day. Couples meet, car-pooling develops, as well as house swapping. Cars with drivers are put in touch with potential customers to the detriment of taxi companies. People needing additional jobs find employment by helping others; some use their network of friends to facilitate improvements. Others launch exchange platforms that sometimes turn into brilliant start-ups. Thus, at the crossroads of current motivations and the many potentials of the computer network, a new complexity is developing which needs no planned installation, but which disrupts our top-down organized systems.

For example, the computer network and the Internet of Things make it possible to continuously observe human populations living their lives and to make use of them for experiments. Medical research is already taking advantage of this opportunity. For example, day-to-day observation of the evolution of symptoms and reactions among diabetics or sufferers of Parkinson's Disease advances our understanding of these diseases.

The society of ordinary people needs to be more aware of itself, of how it works, and how it is evolving. We already have real-time tracking of epidemics, micro-economic and micro-social phenomena, waves of mass emotion or coagulation. If we succeed in accessing deep socio-cultural and socio-economic dimensions through Big Data, we will improve the self-steering capacity of our complex society.

Many "awakened" people feel that our representative and partisan democracies are in fact no longer democracies. They feel that they have no influence on the course of events and that they are entirely controlled by financial interests.

Chapter 7.
From a hyper-financial capitalism to the new socio-economy

Large old companies face the challenge of adapting to a very different environment from the one in which they started. They developed their organization, their culture, their modes of action, and trained their leaders in a hierarchical and pyramidal society - one which was intensely competitive, massive, compartmentalized, stable, simple, bureaucratic, normative, and tutelary. Now they need to learn how to live and manage their development in a radically different and much more demanding horizontal society of ordinary people.

1970S AND 1980S: COMPANIES SEEK TO SUPPORT THE EVOLUTION OF PEOPLE

In the mid-1970s, the climate was changing and the idea of crisis was present in political organizations and many large companies. The first oil crisis erupted. The most dynamic organizations sought to accompany or anticipate changes in people and the social fabric. But companies are regulated by a complex legal framework, with a formal organizational structure and a culture that is change-resistant. The picture of what a good boss, an effective trade unionist, a true leader, or a skilled manager might look like can vary from one country to another, from one company to another, but they are persistent. But in the early 1970s, the leaders of some international companies had the intuition that the world was engaged in radical change (what we call metamorphosis), and wanted to make good use of their socio-perception. For example, Pehr G. Gyllenhammar, president of Volvo, had the intuition that soon Swedish workers would not agree to production line work anymore. In its automotive plants, production lines were replaced by autonomous workshops. At the Anglo-Dutch oil company Royal Dutch Shell, the leaders of strategic planning understood that the world was entering a period of change and that it would be more and more inefficient to plan for the future. Pierre Wack built a network of a few dozen socio-perceptive watchmen all over the world and mobilized two teams of anthropologists with whom they picked out the main socio-cultural currents at work in the world. They began to build evolving scenarios of living socio-economics that enabled Shell to respond to the oil crisis better than its competitors and helped it sense that it would have to behave like a living organism in a new social fabric that seemed about to emerge.

At the beginning of the 1970s, L'Oréal president François Dalle understood that the company needed to remain intensely alive and that relations within it developed more spontaneously than in a rationally organized manner. He was interested in what he called "parallel hierarchies" (what we would call today, "networks that develop spontaneously"). François Dalle encouraged his teams to become fully empathetic and to use them as listening posts to detect changes in the real life of women, which would be useful signals for the future.

These three big companies had among their leaders very empathetic, socio-perceptive, and intuitive personalities who were perfectly at ease in the metamorphosis of the socio-culture. They felt that the future would be very different from the present and that it was necessary to prepare for it. They felt that their staff - not only the senior managers, but also middle rank employees and the shopfloor workers - were real people with their own inner life, and that it was possible to rely on each person's motivations and the sociology of the teams to drive the life of the company.

Some company leaders had perceived that consumers were becoming less susceptible to manipulation, that their expectations were changing, and that the cleverest solution was to bring them genuine satisfaction. In most cases, these were only partial responses to what was in fact a global challenge.

At the same time, marketing became modernized, though without managing to master the new diversity, complexity and fluidity of consumer populations. But by the end of the 1980s, the dialoguing micro-marketing that would take full advantage of the metamorphosis in progress had not yet been invented, and most companies failed to develop symbiosis with their consumers. Observers of socio-cultural change described consumer fatigue, which marketing sought to make up for by increasing advertising pressure or launching price wars.

From the beginning of the 1970s, increasing numbers of students and young executives were looking for jobs that would bring personal fulfillment and a good life. Ten years later, many of them had lost hope of doing so and sought to flourish outside their work.

1990S: THE FINANCIALIZATION OF CAPITALISM HINDERS THE METAMORPHOSIS OF LARGE COMPANIES

Propelled by Ronald Reagan in the United States (1981-1989) and Margaret Thatcher in Britain (1979-1990), a laissez-faire policy allowed a self-organized omnipotent financial system to take over the economy and disrupt or interrupt the adjustment process of many large companies to the new society of people and the accompanying metamorphosis.

Financial circles devised subterfuges and smokescreens to hide what was in effect a casino economy. They committed real crimes that allowed them to enrich themselves at the expense of the real economy. Group shareholders, investment funds, pension funds, hedge funds, banks, and insurance companies, competing with each other to make quick profits, took power on many boards of directors and appointed leaders who, for disproportionate remuneration, served their interests. In doing so, they transformed the culture of many companies, leading them to behave as machines for making the most money possible as fast as possible for their shareholders, rather than as living organisms in the pursuit of healthy long-term development in the world. Financially driven executives were deprived of their sensitivity to the qualitative, to what is human and social, to contact with consumers, and to the demands of a society in metamorphosis.

At a time when consumers need solutions to their real problems, most of these companies have neglected these opportunities. They treated the ecological challenge as an opportunity for short-term communication and not as a real opportunity for development. They preferred to engage in a competition on prices rather than innovation.

They preferred to subcontract work to emerging countries to fuel this competition rather than invest and hire to develop radical or economic innovations. They have tightened the bolts, dismantled successful companies, or fired staff to boost stock prices.

We can distinguish two types of company heads: entrepreneurs and managers. Entrepreneurs, like shopkeepers, appreciate their products and techniques; they like to boost their teams, get their hands dirty, and interact with people, whether staff or customers. Conversely, management types prefer strategic games or mathematics: increase profits and meet or exceed the infamous 15% return on investment required by shareholders. Managers, with their eyes fixed on the figures, treat trained individuals as pawns, subjecting them to harassment, stress, burnout, suicides. Germany has been less disturbed than many of its neighbors by the hyper-financialization of the economy because German managers have technical training, because their family capitalism encourages thinking long term and, finally, because co-management gives employees of German companies a real power to participate in strategic decisions.

Most of the employees in large companies and administrations want to work well and serve their enterprise as well as possible. But many suffer from the imposition of behavioral models, procedures and processes whose meaning they do not understand, or company visions that seem prefabricated. As a result, they are unenthusiastic. Companies do not make full use of the potential for initiative, commitment, creativity, and solidarity of a large proportion of their personnel; meanwhile, empathetic and socio-perceptual people are becoming more numerous. In the interstices of management charts and procedures, spontaneous socio-systems come alive all the more easily as telematics frees communication.

Large companies dominated by short-term finance may have enriched their shareholders and extended their influence, but they emerged from crisis without having prepared for their future. They did not anticipate the innovations that would work in today's world. They have damaged their strategic skills, their human balance, their social capital, their resilience and, ultimately, their vital prognosis. At the same time, they fueled unemployment and increased inequality. They have made people despair and have nurtured opposition to the elites and powers in place.

They present an obstacle to the adaptation of business and the economy to the new society of people, thus contributing to the damage of the Western economic and strategic position in the world.

These firms did not sense that the development of the society of people had increased the demands on companies, asking them - as well as the public authorities - to take care of the society in which they lived, to cure its sufferings and its pathologies rather than add to them, to contribute to the common good and the care of the environment. They have not responded to this demand. However, after the great crisis, some businesses immersed in the new socio-economy began to open up to metamorphosis.

2010-2020: SOME LARGE COMPANIES ARE OPENING TO METAMORPHOSIS

Willy-nilly, in the second decade of the century, large companies are opening to metamorphosis.

From a hyper-financial capitalism to the new socio-economy

Western capitalism can neither anticipate nor handle crises. The financial crisis that came from America in 2007 and 2008 has turned into a major economic crisis. States saved financial capitalism with public money: the people's money. Crowds of Americans and Spaniards have lost their homes. Unemployment hit hard in Europe and the United States. The sufferings have accumulated.

Opinion quickly mobilized. Here and there, we realized that companies treated their staff poorly and laid off personnel in order to pay their shareholders better. In the late 2000s, a collective wave of anti-finance and anti-business intelligence emerged. The feeling spread that we were at a tipping point. The economic and financial system and the big companies seemed to be unable to stay as they were.

By the beginning of 2010, the phenomenon had become massive and finally reached the establishment. Here and there leaders said that a radical change had become a vital challenge, insisting on the need for companies to fully comply with their societal functions as well as their economic ones if they were to survive. Graduates of top US business schools take a solemn oath, like Hippocrates, to give priority in their professional activities to social well-being, not profit. For their part, many staff members want their management to think less about finance and shareholders and more about business, innovation and new developments. The financialization of capitalism and the disproportionately high remuneration of top managers are blamed for a loss of involvement within the company.

Nevertheless, the financial lobbies remain powerful. Faced with strategic choices for the company, it is still too often short-term financial profitability that tips the balance in one direction rather than another. We are still talking about stock market redundancies. The new fact is that these moves pass less and less unnoticed and are increasingly the cause of indignation.

Managers who are becoming more socio-perceptive realize that their company does not have all the skills which are indispensable in today's world, such as sensing changing needs, innovating, developing new forms of leadership, detecting timely cooperation, etc.

The paths of these leaders are varied. Some staff are aware of the global challenge: they make their diagnoses - possibly with the help of consultants; they develop their skills and an organizational and training road map to confront the challenge. Some create or wake up socio-analytic cells to reveal opportunities and threats.

Even in the absence of awareness and management decisions, many companies are dragged into the process of metamorphosis. Indeed, every company is immersed in the global society and is deeply penetrated by it; a growing proportion of its staff and managers are autonomous and far-sighted and connected to the networks of the new socio-economy. They are, without expressly wishing it, the carriers of a biological process of transformation that nobody leads and which emanates from the intimate mechanisms of the organism.

Associations, think tanks, foundations, networks, a large number of consultants and a growing population of coaches have given themselves the mission of encouraging and helping companies to make their transformation happen. They involve companies in programs, in cooperatives or in the ecosystems that transform them.

Today, young executives are particularly active and worry many senior managements. To live as they wish, to find meaning and flourish, they unravel the old rationally organized economy compartmentalized by the elite. Their personality is not fundamentally different from that of their parents; however, instead of dreaming, they dare to say, "let us do it!"

In the company and around it, among its staff and its interlocutors, as in global society, the hierarchical continues to weaken as the pyramidal social fabric crumbles. Skilled managers who can rely on the experience and motivations of their staff are more likely to get their way and get good results than those who impose their authority; in the long run, they succeed better and are positively selected. Many have found that attitudes of influence are more successful than authoritarian attitudes. They seek to learn, and succeed better than those who do not perceive the meaning of evolution. Managers who have become skilled socio-perceptives are able to discern the social contexts in which it is more efficient to adopt influential behaviors or authoritarian behaviors. Their performances show the results. Leaders identify the success of influential behaviors and organize themselves to promote them. Training centers, seminars, consultants, and coaches that teach the "new leadership" - i.e. influence-based leadership - are multiplying.

On the wave of humanist metamorphosis, employees seek to find meaning in their work. They may react against being treated as pawns or seeing their colleagues or collaborators trapped in bureaucratic procedures. Sometimes they see that they are not alone: others in the company may have the same problem. When they discover each other, a network begins to form. And it may be that a socio-perceptive manager becomes aware of the phenomenon and understands that the company can encourage and take advantage of it. These socio-perceptive change agents thus play a considerable role. Humanist and pragmatic, they disrupt prevailing mental models and become powerful vectors of transformation. They give life to informal networks that tend to make the business more responsive to its own functioning and to its relationship to this or that aspect of its ecosystem. With or without the blessing of top management, their intervention brings out islands - even archipelagos - of spontaneity, shared vision, participation, and meaning in companies where purely rational organization is still well established.

Even when piloted by a specialized cell, the transformation of these learning and agile companies takes the form of a tentative journey rather than an orchestrated action. Proceeding by trial and error and corrections, they offer the opportunity to company officers and employees to continue to feed their human sensitivity and empathy. They allow them to learn to anticipate the evolutionary trends of living systems, probable futures, and significant scenarios, and to practice tentative strategies. Beyond simplifying hierarchies and developing horizontal relationships, these companies explore different forms of heterarchy, with authority changing hands depending on the circumstances. They practice co-leadership and test collective decision-making processes. They flee bureaucratic procedures and cultivate spontaneous life. They behave like living organisms, sustaining their vitality by embracing the dynamics and opportunities of their social body and their environment.

Their "leaders" are less committed to making decisions and to controlling than to ensuring that organically developed regulations work properly and that sound directions are taken. Their head office and staff realize that the global socio-economy is changing and that it is urgent to anticipate. They devise strategies to enable them to take advantage of the current restructuring. These companies know that the products, services, machines, and distribution methods operating in ten years will be very different from those of today. They feel out processes to stimulate innovation. Some seek to involve the entire social body in the production of promising ideas. Others create small specialized teams to sample metamorphosis; these remain detached and serve as scouts.

More and more businesses are drawn into collaborations and ecosystems where they interact with other businesses, associations, NGOs and, sometimes, public bodies. They change their nature and become new hybrid collectivities.

Danone societal reorientation

In the early 2000s, taking stock of its new environment, Danone[33] effected a radical societal reorientation, relying on a mix of strategic opportunism and the vision of its management.

Strategic opportunism was Danone's response to takeover risks from giants like Pepsi, Coca Cola or Nestlé. By differentiating itself through health, Danone protects itself against the producers of chocolate bars, sugary drinks or salty snacks, accused of being among the main sources responsible for the rise of the obesity in the world. Franck Riboud shares with his father, Antoine Riboud, the founder of BSN (Danone since 1994), a socio-perceptive capacity that allows visionary bosses to perceive early warning signals of socio-cultural change. In the early 2000s, a growing vigilance towards big brands was led by the media, consumers and NGOs. This development had a strong impact on Danone's actions in terms of food safety,

---

33. Jérôme Tubiana, *La Saga Danone*, JCLattes, 2015

environmental protection, employment and respect for human rights in emerging countries. The objective is to "bring health through food to the greatest number". In 2006, Grameen Danone was created with Professor Yunus in Bangladesh, and later Danone Communities.

Thus emerges an outline of a company that will be at home in the metamorphosed socio-economy. It will be less an autonomous and self-serving player, than an element of one or more eco-socio-systems, participating in a distributed governance, and contributing to the smooth functioning of the society-as-a-brain.

The financialization of capitalism isolated economic leaders who were enriched by the suffering middle class. It slowed the humanist metamorphosis and could have blocked it. Perhaps it was the 2007 crisis that allowed the metamorphosis process to regain its influence on the big old companies.

The bifurcation point is also that of a new capitalism immersed in the digital revolution. Will the metamorphosis be preserved? In the era of artificial intelligence, how will the society of ordinary people react?

Chapter 8.
The digital revolution: from the portable computer to "Artificial Intelligence"

The digital development that appeared more than 70 years ago was a revolution as important as the appearance of writing. In the twenty-first century, the extremely rapid development of the Web, mobile phones and social networks is catapulting many developing countries into metamorphosis.

THE WEB AND PORTABLE PHONES ARE TRANSFORMING THE WORLD

Sixteen million people had access to the Internet in 1995, 36 million in 1996, 300 million in 2000, 1 billion in 2005, 2 billion in 2011, more than 4 billion in 2018, about 54% of the world's population. In January 2018, 73% in America, 80% in Europe, 34% in Africa, 48% in South-East Asia. The most developed countries are the best connected, but the others are catching up quickly, with a connection rate in 2018 of more than 60% Morocco or Tunisia[34].

In developing countries, the process of installing the Internet may be the opposite of what it was in the West.

---

34. BDM 2018/08/29

Micro-telecommunication systems are often set up in socio-cultures that are still hierarchical, codified or massed in groups, favoring the development of varied and horizontal personal communications, which give individual personalities a chance to evolve. It is not uncommon for people to see their autonomy increasing, as in China, without having had to make the effort to emancipate themselves, but simply because they use these new tools. A society of people becomes aware of its existence and its strength. Rural areas in Africa, China, India and even Russia were cut off by their geographical isolation from the influence of social metamorphosis and from practical sources of information. For them, digital evolution is beginning a process of emancipation. African women can participate in programs and forums. Muslim women can chat with each other on social media independent of their husbands.

Of the billions of people with mobile phones in 2012, several billion were in developing countries. We have never seen an innovation become globalized so quickly. Mobile phones are changing the lives of more people faster than any other technical innovation. And it is in developing countries that the change is the most spectacular. The World Bank estimates that in a typical African country, a 10% growth in the number of mobile phones induces an increase of 0.8% of GDP. In cases like Kenya where the local system allows the use of mobile phones to transfer money, local economic life is transformed, increasing the income of user households by 5% to 30%. The Arab Spring revolts in Tunisia, Egypt and elsewhere would probably never have been able to develop or acquire such strength in such a short time without laptops and networks.

INFORMATION TECHNOLOGIES ARE A SOURCE OF LIFE

The combined development of our humanizing skills and our information technology is a source of increased strength.

One of the main triggers of humanistic metamorphosis was the reopening in the middle of the last century of our emotional-relational and spiritual intelligences, and the beginning of their dialogue with our rational intelligence. We now understand living society better. We assume our independence. We develop our skills of empathy, socio-perception, and anticipation. Spectacular advances in computing can be combined with amplified human skills to help us achieve a major leap in social complexity.

Thirsting for independence: laptops, the internet of things, the multifunction telephone

The extremely rapid development of digital information systems has challenged us with a change of scale. In the mid-1980s, the use of microcomputers and their interconnection were effectively imposed; this led to the use of connected microcomputer networks, reinforcing the need for emancipation and connection, dramatically accelerating the development of networks and socio-systems, and increasing the influence of ordinary people in all walks of life. People became able to search for and process the information they needed independently. The development of Internet technologies in the late 1960s was also inspired by the desire for freedom from the specialized military circles that had conceived a fundamentally non-hierarchical network structure. As the Internet began to spread, there emerged in the United

Part III. A great bifurcation

States the subculture of "hackers", particularly at the Massachusetts Institute of Technology. These young hackers diverted the Internet from its original military vocation to horizontal communication from person to person (peer to peer).

A phenomenal amount of data about people, their actions and behaviors can now be collected, linked, analyzed, interpreted, and used extremely quickly. This is Big Data. Advances in computing also allow for instant access to a great deal of information about people, things, and events: the Internet of Things. Personal computers are less and less on people's desktops, and more and more in their pocket or their bag, connecting them personally and permanently to interactive networks. It is the smartphone or tablet that potentially connects all people in real time to each other and to all networks. Geolocation makes it possible to locate any event and every communicator in space and to follow its path. The 3D printer offers opportunities for production decentralization and individualization.

Use of the Web has become second nature to a growing portion of the population, especially young people. They are permanently connected through a smartphone or tablet that never leaves them, locates them, and ensures they are fully connected and can react instantly. They are increasingly informed about what concerns them. They can participate in self-regulation in real time.

Big data scares us. We fear that organizations will exploit our personal data at our expense or use it to manipulate us; that we will find ourselves embarrassingly confronted with our past; that some skilled Big Data holders will become too powerful; that entire chunks of data will be known only by a few categories of operator who will use them as tools for dominance.

Indeed, the "progress" of neuroscience could lead to the development of techniques for the mass or selective manipulation of populations. If society does not realize this in time to react, we could find ourselves back in a civilization based on tamed or domesticated men and women, functioning once more on a hierarchical principle.

Regulation to protect the metamorphosis currently underway

Spontaneous power surges capable of distorting regulation within society are probably a permanent threat to the process of metamorphosis if counterbalancing powers or new regulatory systems do not emerge in time. The previous technological revolution saw start-up companies in California that, in a few years, have become global giants. Some of them control information (Big Data) and, soon, systems of self-regulation that could give them excessive power and could disrupt the societal democracy towards which we are moving. This was the case when finance took precedence over the economy, when the free play of self-organized markets could allow a dangerous disruptor of the metamorphosis process to take hold. The American giants of the Internet are in conflict with Brussels and several European governments, who fear they will take too much power. Cambridge Analytica and Facebook's troubles with the US Congress seem to show that, not only public authorities, but perhaps the society of people will in future be able to generate countervailing powers. We saw that even very small structures can bring giants to self-regulation. The power of California's Silicon

Valley could prompt the installation in China, Europe, India, and elsewhere of competing or opposing powers.

Several paths open to us*:* that of society-as-anthill, in which the mass of humanity will act more or less automatically, and that of society-as-a-brain, in which flexibly interconnected human groups co-create a collectively chosen future.

SOCIETY-AS-ANT-HILL: A FRIGHTENING FUTURE

Artificial intelligence in the hands of a few oligarchs

Dominated by robots, a few human oligarchs, scientists, bankers, or politicians could lay hands on scientific discoveries and advances, leaving the rest of the world an anthill of odd-job humans.

Data worship

Humanity could be divided into a few "experts", whose life is artificially and indefinitely prolonged, and "useless" humans, replaced little by little by robots. This is a return to the scientistic dreams of the nineteenth century, with undefined techno-scientific progress expressed as the dream of Immortal Man. To do away with death has always been man's dream, ever since the Babylonian Gilgamesh and up to modern medical science. At the turn of the seventeenth century, Francis Bacon considered the possibility of prolonging life and the emergence of new species.

The convergence of rapid advances in genetics, biotechnology, neuroscience, computing and nanotechnology, currently provides inspiration for Californian transhumanism laboratories. They look forward to a transformed human being, augmented by artificial intelligence and robots, dominating death. They seem to be embroiled in a Prometheus delirium which, in its present form, is the opposite of the humanist metamorphosis.

It is possible that the search for transhumanist dreams, if they escape whistleblowers and spiritual and social thought police, could lead to the development of hybrid human-machine beings or the creation of artificial intelligence systems and robots that could escape the control of their designers. The conflict that has begun to develop between the proponents of transhumanism and those looking to a humanized science or spirit of metamorphosis could become crucial.

The reign of algorithms and men-machines

Among the prophets of this distressing future is Yuval Noah Harari, who envisions a society dominated by Big Data, without doctors, lawyers or artists, who will have been replaced by computers. This future includes the driverless automobile governed by a computer implementing programmed ethical choices (should it crush the pregnant woman or the cyclist?), in which the voice of humanism seems reduced or absent.

This new religion is dataism. Harari[35] tells us, "As belief in the individual crumbles and authority is invested in algorithms, the humanist vision of the world - based on individual choice, democracy and the free market - will

---

35. Harari, *Homo Deus*, Albin Michel, 2017.

become obsolete". But does the humanistic vision rest on individual choice and the free market, or rather on the fulfillment of the person and the democracy of the common good? Harari's declaration[36] is a warning. It is clear that formerly, one said "the brain is like a computer", but living individuals and society are infinitely more complex, made of disorder and regeneration. Living organisms are not algorithms. They are "open" with a variability that characterizes their evolution.

Could artificial intelligence escape its designers? Transhumanist views are varied. Basically, the goal is the immortality of the human being, by combining our own life with the necessary machines.

As a first stage we can speak of "the augmented man", but the followers of transhumanism go further and seek immortality. Extropianism is based on faith in unlimited progress through science and technology. The Europeans, with Nick Bostrom, are more techno-progressive, although the concept of "superintelligence" - machines copying the human brain ever more efficiently - takes us down the same path. Elon Musk, the founder of Space X, links transhumanism to the economic dimension of our social evolution. Here we are far from the human dimension of metamorphosis.

If technical progress is at the center of culture, progress cannot be stopped. But our observation of society leads us along a completely different path.

---

36. Interview "l'Observateur", 2017/09/10.

SOCIETY-AS-A-BRAIN: ARTIFICIAL INTELLIGENCE AS AN OPPORTUNITY

AI, indispensable in an increasingly complex world

A foreseeable concrete future: AI, digitalization, is one of the elements of the current metamorphosis and can help with the search for the common good. Awareness of "the madness of science" has developed throughout the twentieth century, generating questions about nuclear energy, and the perverse effects of medical, agricultural, and industrial techniques, for example. This is salutary and has led to a whole apparatus of precautions, the creation of ethics committees, and a global awareness of the spirit of nature. The risks mentioned now seem less catastrophic because there is a good chance that Homo Sapiens will resist being carried away.

Let us repeat that probably for the first time in the history of humanity, Homo Sapiens actually uses its rational, emotional-relational, sensory and spiritual intelligences at the same time. And this gives it a considerable primacy over the machine. If our metamorphosis is protected, if it is not monopolized by power lobbyists, human intelligence will be helped - not submerged - by artificial intelligence. This is because the metamorphosis puts living ecology at the center of everything.

"Artificial intelligence is aptly named: it is an intelligence made by computer techniques, so there is no reason to think that it is thinking[37]". By contrast, human intelligence refers to thought experiments carried out in the labs of the mind. More and more decisions are not made, but

---
37. Étienne Klein, Revue Noosphère, Mars 2018.

rather offered, by machines. For example, when you are in your car with your GPS, you make the final decision: you choose your route.

Digital technology is needed today to help us better understand the complex elements of our ecosystem. In thinking metamorphosis, let us observe in a new context, with new glasses, profoundly humanistic experiments.

The legal and medical professions will change: lawyers and doctors will become information catalysts. Digital tools will conduct the analyses, allowing them to devote themselves to decision-making, humanistic, and psychological dimensions, where their socio-perception, empathy, and intuition will allow them to help the one who is no longer a client or patient, but a participant in therapeutic decision-making. When an illness appears, this co-actor will consult both the Internet to learn more, and a doctor to choose among the different paths possible and accompany the patient. Robots are not made for that.

In a balanced society, AI will help to better identify the "common goods" needed. This is a major political, social, and economic issue. This is all necessary current research. Beyond the techno-scientific myth, we focus on the human. We live in complexity and unpredictability; we have said goodbye to simple extrapolation; we are now thinking and acting at the point where civilization branches.

Artificial intelligence, networks and metamorphosis, Hackers, Hackathon

Digital communication enables people to be networked, and gives them the tools for everything collaborative, from carpooling to co-production. Fab Labs, lab spaces where you can co-create any object from a table to a mobile phone ("third places", making available shared digital technical elements, robots, 3D printers, etc.), are based above all on cooperation among people, creating collective intelligence, and innovating together. The space-makers (see box below), are places where street innovation and the hand of man can reinvent adaptability and know-how.

Thanh Nghiem[38], crazy toads, street-wise innovation: David Li

Crazy toads are those who, to reach their pond and breed during the mating season, do not cross roads with the attendant risk of being crushed by cars but look for another way, in this case the small tunnels created for them by humans. These toads that reject their ancestral routine are the image of innovators in our metamorphosis. Thanh Nghiem finds them in the larger world, where the crazy toad is the deviant who saves the species and makes others aware of dangers that threaten them.

An example of a crazy toad working in the larger field is David Li. He had the idea of studying street developments in Shenzhen, where innovation is developed for and by the people. He postulated that we can open up the production on the Internet, and David Li's teams created a robot that works unaided to remove weeds, using artificial intelligence to differentiate weeds from useful plants. This allows humans to manage organic vegetable production without breaking their backs.

By creating a platform, Shenzhen Open Innovation Lab, David Li has enabled anyone to prototype all sorts of objects: smartphones, drones, electric vehicles, etc. In France, Wiko has become the second largest

---

38. Thanh Nghiem and Cedric Villani, *The Mad Toad Manifesto*, Paris, Massot, 2017.

telephone producer in less than a year, thanks to this system.

David Li is the Robin Hood of modern times, who wants to work for the general good of all on the principle of "Goods for good".

New cultures are appearing: are hackers pirates or handymen who want to share? As the meaning of the terms used changes, as do the lenses we look through. The "hackathon" - a cross between a hack and a marathon - is a gathering that quickly produces clever new things. The goal is sharing, giving: another conception of society. From this perspective, the hacker is someone who wants to be a master of things that he uses. A true hacker will develop his knowledge to the maximum, become a virtuoso in his field, and, especially, share his knowledge with others and be recognized by his peers. He does not support pyramidal hierarchic systems in companies or governments.

What are the limits, what self-regulation is necessary to take care of the living environment, what new forms of education must we develop in the face of these issues?

AI AND EDUCATION

Shared learning - the internal ability of a company's members to learn from each other - is the key challenge for civilization. To develop it, we can rely on data received from forms of artificial intelligence re-analyzed by Collective Intelligence. This is the challenge facing the "learning society" launched in France in 2017-18, whose origins we can trace to the Society for Organizational

Learning, SoL[39], born at MIT in 1998. In a complex and flexible environment, each of the cells of learning organizations interconnect, learning together as in a living organism.

> **SoL, Man at the centre of organizations, "Dare to metamorphose"**
>
> For twenty years, SoL has focused its research and actions on a new approach to management: "Dare to metamorphose" was the theme of the global forum organized in 2014, where 450 people from 50 countries on 50 projects met in Paris. Such a planetary event was only possible through new means of digital communication, the interaction of networks, collective intelligence, etc. The Dialogues of Learning[40] gave practical illustrations of the implementation of this philosophy and these approaches, and the central role of shared learning throughout life thanks to new means of communication.

The metamorphosis of education: Developing one's socio-perception

The accent in education is on the *process* and *skill in living*, rather than on the accumulation of knowledge made permanently available through AI. This is a lifelong process of individual and collective learning that allows systemic thinking, integrating the side effects and interactions of any decision, to create a shared global vision of the goal to achieve. This is the central goal of the work on socio-perception that we talked about. The youth and the adult

---

39. SoL, the Society for Organizational Learning, Peter Senge, *The 5th discipline*, Eyrolles 2016.
40. Béatrice Arnaud, Corinne Ejeil, *Guide to the Learning Organization* (Fr), Eyrolles, 2018.

perceive their environment, they learn to adapt to it. AI will give them the data, but it is up to them to know how to create concepts, to associate them, to work on short or long processes, delays in adaptation and the notion of time: "Learning to put time first, this is initiating processes rather than possessing spaces[41].

Other forms of education: Systemic thinking in the education of young people in Holland, the meeting of education and business.

Systemic thought is habitual in the young child until the age of 12 to 14. Thereafter, puberty and education cause him to lose it. How can we preserve this habitual childhood faculty? Experiments in schools in the Netherlands[42] have shown that 12-year-olds can respond to industrial management problems posed by small businesses and can imagine scenarios; they have received the data, they communicate in a network, together and in a systemic way, and thus are able to sketch out concrete future paths.

In its report on the Learning Society, the French Centre de Recherches Interdisciplinaires relies on work in the field and organizes various experiments, such as the Savanturiers - doctoral students who carry out applied research with primary and secondary schoolchildren.

What will be the school of the future? Homo Sapiens is short-sighted, it cannot describe it. But the tracks are there. AI will help, but the self-regulation of a living society must be established to make the new contributions beneficial,

---

41. Pope Francis, Evangelii Gaudium.
42. Guus Geisen, Autopoiesis, De Lerende School, Netherlands.

to develop independence as regards the AI machine, to keep human intelligence - emotional, relational, spiritual - in its place, serving our social metamorphosis. This self-regulation comes through socio-perception, discernment, empowerment, and so through a form of education. Social metamorphosis is the preservation of meaning. "If robots are capable of doing human jobs, it's because human jobs have been robotized[43]".

During 1990-2000, computers were installed on the desks of those who could use the fabulous facilities of the internet; faced with this new tool, however, very little global education was achieved. Spam and trolling spread without the introduction of any inferential ladder allowing the user to come down to earth[3] before the damage done to ordinary reading and writing becomes too serious! Artificial intelligence requires a basic humanist training that specifically includes education in the acceptance or refusal of choices put forward by a machine.

Do we accept or refuse the choice of route proposed by our GPS? "I also want to relax in a park, visit a cathedral, have a meal in a good restaurant..." In Man-Machine relations, leaving space for feelings and humanist awareness is a choice that is an essential part of education.

METAMORPHOSIS AND ARTIFICIAL INTELLIGENCE ARE COMPLEMENTARY

This is probably new in the history of Homo Sapiens. Developing his natural socio-perception, ensuring a permanent interaction between "his four brains"- rational, emotional, sensory and spiritual - Homo Sapiens will make

---

43. Étienne Klein

use of what we can call artificial Intelligence. Our outlook is methodologically optimistic, based on self-organization of the living ecosystem. In the box below Pierre Giorgini[44] provides a counterpoint. These two approaches are the basis for an indispensable discussion.

Can artificial intelligence promote positive metamorphosis or, on the contrary, restrict it?

by Pierre Giorgini, President-Rector of the Catholic University of Lille

Who can deny that the fundamentals of civilization (hierarchies, proximities, and borders) are being disturbed by the ongoing humanist metamorphosis which Alain de Vulpian tells us is beneficial, as people become more autonomous, more insightful, better able to trace their personal paths in an increasingly complex environment? Indeed, out of the social fabric - masses and packets of standardized types of individuals - come interactions between networks of people, changing and self-organizing each in their own way; hierarchy and the domestication of man by man are becoming more relaxed; cooperation now outweighs competition. For Alain de Vulpian, this is a gift from heaven or the result of an innate intelligence of living society. His optimism goes so far as to think that this metamorphosis is preparing us to meet the deadly ecological and geopolitical challenges that our rationalist madness has accumulated.

But others, such as Bernard Stiegler or Dominique Cardon, rightly observe that digital entropy is pushing us towards a generalized disorder where ephemeral and instantaneous connections reign, preventing the development of sustainable, shared and dynamic corpora of knowledge, in addition to generalized learning.

In their opinion, any networked technical components (technosphere) endowed with so-called artificial

---

44. Pierre Giorgini, *La tentation d'Eugénie*, Bayard , 2018

intelligence and interactive capacities independent of human mediation, equipped with multiple connections and instantaneous feedback, would develop independently as a social fabric, overshadowing human capacity and tending to dominate it. The value produced would be captured by the dominant economic, state and military powers, who would hold back open source options and prepare to use the exosphere as a weapon of mass influence.

We risk being enclosed in a double helix of accelerated entropic degradation due to the autonomization of the technical sphere by digital technology, which escapes and destroys social linkages instead of reinforcing them in their diversity and autopoietic capacity[45]. The exosphere's immense capacities for targeted influence (think of Cambridge Analytica) would be put at the service of the traditional issues of domination.

The Internet initially carried the hope of an open world, of collective knowledge shared in co-development. But the "Wikiworld" has been turned around because of what Bernard Stiegler calls the massification of mimetic behavior. This leads to an accelerated depletion of resources and diversity, both natural resources but also those of the collective knowledge of our time[46].

All in all, it is not impossible that metamorphosis be curbed, put at the service of the outdated dynamics of domination, forcing mankind to endure some major collapses before a freer, non-hierarchical alternative can develop.

Applying the norms and standards of the industrial economy to the digital economy amounts to transforming a remedy into a devastating poison: overcapitalization; value captured by capitalist monsters; destruction of the commons and the common good; development of zones of lawlessness where value is destroyed without any true creative

---

45. An autopoietic system is a system that in an unstable environment has the ability to constantly reinvent its internal processes to adapt to the environment. It is this characteristic of what is living which makes it possible to obtain quasi-stable systems in entropic instability.
46. Michel Foucault, *Les mots et les choses* (Words and Things).

input. Our inability to reappraise the revolution of artificial intelligence and indeed metamorphosis as a gift from heaven, transforms this human development into a formidable poison when it is approached with the norms of industrial society, its regimes of financial domination, and its regulatory systems.

A bifurcation must and can occur to avoid this, opening up tremendous hopes consistent with Alain de Vulpian's optimism. It can originate and grow in the midst of these technical advances, leading to a cognitive increase capable of meeting the challenges we face: solutions that are co-created and mastered by real, ordinary people.

Low cost solutions developed by and for the makers of metamorphosis are already multiplying (crazy toads, street innovation, communities of economic resilience, third places and social surroundings). To amplify and accelerate this movement, four conditions are essential in my opinion:

1. Promote open source AI support platforms to the status of common good of humanity, at least at the European level. Put AI at the service of local creativity. This must be supported by research managed and financed by a public civic authority.

2. Reconnect the needs of real people to reality, with products and services they support in a co-developed, repairable, sustainable and low-cost perspective.

3. Support deliberations at the local level, accompanied by action research to construct knowledge - epistemes of use and manufacturing - networked at the global level and connected to the challenges facing the planet, in a collaborative learning perspective.

4. Network actors and create a parliament of consciousnesses at the global level, opposed to the privatization of creative platforms, which are the shared possession of what belongs to the common good, viewed as the heritage of humanity.

These four principles apply even more to what concerns living society and genetic manipulation. In a nutshell,

> the goal is to build a society made up of overlapping, self-adjusting, and networked learning communities, which have taken control of their destinies at the local and global levels, and are concerned for the common good, including the elements of our shared humanity. Are we on this path?

Metamorphosis is based on cooperation and empathy. Transhumanism is about singularity, a surge of technology; metamorphosis is about otherness. What about complementarity?

Are we going towards the triumph of one or the other tendency, towards a synthesis of the two, or towards a coexistence opposing Europe to America? If we consider the previous stages of humanistic metamorphosis, the coupling of both - that is to say the fruitful interaction of technical progress with shaping trends in socio-cultural evolution - seems to us the most likely scenario.

For example, in 1900, the automobile - individually manufactured by highly specialized workers - seemed a means of locomotion for the rich and not a powerful factor for socio-cultural acceleration. But it became so from the moment Henry Ford introduced mass production lines, cost reduction and an increase in wages, which allowed workers to buy a car. The automobile became the symbol of a society where everyone felt free to travel and independently mobile. Similarly, computer science, in the beginning, was embodied by powerful central computers linked hierarchically to large structures. Digitization only became a major vector of metamorphosis when it was able to respond to the enormous hunger for interpersonal connections in the 1980s through interconnected microcomputers and the internet. Can we hope for similar developments between scientific transhumanism and humanistic metamorphosis?

Digitization must be seen as one of the elements of current metamorphosis. It would not have spread so widely in the absence of the Internet and networks. Young people feel this complementarity and are at ease with it, while preserving, as we said, their values and their search for a society based on meaning. Today a crowd of ordinary, socio-perceptive people, new collectives and a growing number of companies and political actors are aware of the importance of digital communication in the development of social metamorphosis. At the same time, they perceive the structural threats and, more or less consciously, want to take care of humanist metamorphosis. Very varied "Happymorphosis" networks are rising here and there and interconnecting. This is the society of tomorrow.

However "society-as-a-brain", the socio-economy of the common good, and social democracy, are not yet ripe. We do not know how or what to do.

How can we take into account the life of each citizen and each network without asking them to formally formulate an opinion which will, by its very formulation, be subject to manipulation? How can we evaluate contributions of different socio-economic actors to the common good? How can we identify pathological deviations early enough? If we encourage work in this direction, Big Data and AI systems can help. Algorithms will have to be invented to answer these questions.

An electronic post-representative democracy?

The combination of Big Data and the Internet of Things (throwing in a dose of artificial intelligence and living human intuition) seems to be able to provide a decisive aid to the optimizing self-regulation of hypercomplex systems, which are too complex to be processed by laws and procedures. It is likely that in coming years we will manufacture artificial self-regulating ecosystems, artifacts that will come to life by producing an improvement, as smart grids do today. They could for example aim to reduce unemployment in a given area, or reduce school failure in a student population, optimize traffic circulation in a town, or even optimize the situation of a company and its personnel within their ecosystems. This approach could pave the way for an electronic post-representative democracy - all the more so since the current sphere of politics and representative democracy are cut off from living society.

Chapter 9.
Towards a participative democracy

The democracy we know today is inherited from the eighteenth and nineteenth centuries. But society has changed. Our representative, partisan, bureaucratic democracies can no longer respond to the extreme level of complexity of our society.

REPRESENTATIVE DEMOCRACY REACHES A DEAD END

In 2015, in "In praise of metamorphosis, on the march to a new humanity[47]", we wrote:

"The representative and partisan democracy that we practice is at odds with the new society, which feels excluded from power and is beginning to challenge its legitimacy". The authoritarian and bureaucratic governance we have inherited becomes ineffective and produces turbulence when it operates in a hyper-complex and well-functioning society. The resulting poor governance leads people to react against the governing classes. The system of a tutelary state and uniform social protection built in the middle of the twentieth century is crumbling, but only

---

[47]. Digital edition, Chapter 12, download epub www.happymorphose.com

slowly, running contrary to a society that today aims to optimize the particular situation of each person. The European Union falls between two stools and is paralyzed. Because of these misalignments, the governments of the EU and most of our countries are ineffective and unable to properly support our development in the context of ongoing globalization. They do not provide the common good that a people's society expects. Our populations are suffering and are demoralized. They accuse the ruling elites, both national and European, of being responsible for their misfortune, and brutally challenge them in the polls and in the street. Serious political crises could disrupt the metamorphosis".

In Europe and the United States, the new society of people self-organizes and orientates itself, but it has not yet given birth to a new democratic government that meets this level of complexity. The process of emergence of a societal democracy is already well under way, but it is slowed down by resistance, new challenges, fears, and the slowness of transformation of earlier powers in all forms.

Erasing ideologies and parties

Will we agree to be represented today? Inefficient governments contribute to the opposition of part of the population to the governing authorities and parties. Most elections give rise to head-on oppositions between right-wing and left-wing candidates. The right tends to be for free enterprise and bosses, the left for workers and redistribution.

In both cases, while believing the general interest is being served, we do not see the complex reality as it is and we advocate uninformed policies that do not take into account the systemic situation, interactions, and side effects. And yet, in the society of ordinary people, partisan divisions are blurring.

Unemployment, the reception of immigrants, societal problems, and the protection of the planet, divide both the right and the left. The financialization of the economy widens the gap between the popular masses and the leaders.

But the practices of the political class remain dominated by the mental model of the party battle and majority power. Doubt is spreading in our countries concerning the virtues of representative and partisan democracy: Do they not tend to encourage parliamentarians and leaders to focus on the short term, on their reelection or reappointment, thus diverting them from essential strategic reflections for the medium and long term? In elections, the number of abstentions is growing, while votes for populist parties are increasing in all countries.

The political class is a relatively closed environment where only parliamentarians, activists and specialized journalists meet. They see each other, talk to each other. They stylize the clashes which form their stock-in-trade, making theatrical events out of political life. But the idea eludes them that the society of people and the new socio-economy needs careful oversight capable of triggering therapeutic interventions. Most politicians or political journalists are interested only in political theater. Neither seem to know what ordinary people are going through.

Among the latter, many feel alienated and criticize this politicizing outlook; the universe of theatrical politics and that of the society of people tend to exist separately. Journalists and politicians alike connect to social networks. They broadcast opinions and observe those of others -

mainly messages from political personalities or extremists; they remain as yet unable to tap into Big Data to learn about the fluctuations in our collective intelligence and the evolution of the life of our societies. What could be the new form of democracy desired by the society of people?

Future democracy will tend to be less representative and more participatory and implicit

One could feel represented as a specifically categorized individual, but not once one has become an autonomous and changing socio-perceptive person, capable of decoding the manipulative effects of communication and false news. Such aware people may want to participate more in the preparation of decisions, or to implement them, rather than be decision-makers themselves; they hope thus to preserve their freedom. In France in 2017, the "En Marche" movement enabled its activists to take part in developing programs. Mechanisms may perhaps emerge, particularly at the local level, which would involve citizens in change and in reducing deficits in the common good.

A society of people in which "new hybrid animals" and eco-socio-systems can emerge will be too complex for partisan and bureaucratic governance to manage, let alone to produce the common good for the people, which has to be distinguished from top-down general interest decisions. This implies a catalytic governance that frees and de-bureaucratizes the socio-economy, while ensuring that protective or self-therapeutic systems emerge. In this perspective, the new deputies would be less appointed representatives and more facilitators-leaders of the involvement and participation of the people.

Towards a new leadership that will be able to catalyze innovations

In our countries, hierarchical governance traditionally knows where it wants to go and imposes laws, plans and procedures to achieve its purpose. But a living and hyper-complex society whose hierarchical reflex is crumbling cannot be commanded. The goal of a hierarchical structure will no longer apply, but this does not mean that there will be no leadership; it will simply have changed in nature. Good governance will become catalytic: it will know which among desirable evolutions or essential cures can emerge naturally and by what paths. The catalyst-leader will intervene lightly to stimulate desirable innovations while maintaining balance, like a musical conductor.

Bureaucratic organization, with its formalized processes, categories and pre-established hierarchies, clashes with autonomous, living persons who could otherwise have mobilized their energies. The blossoming of a living Europe, for example, is blocked by its bureaucratic governance. Technological innovations are often born in garages or back rooms. The new state governance will probably be born on the sidewalks of cities, in the regions, and will be the product of hybrid organisms combining pieces of collective movements formerly in conflict or belonging to different "species" - public and private sectors, civil society, spiritual sector, etc. Hybridization is, at the moment, one of the most promising paths to metamorphosis. Public governance bodies need to hybridize to find new efficiencies. Examples will be given.

Towards a "glocal" governance

Governance will tend to become "glocal", that's to say both local and global. The local level is critical. At this level, it is easier to experiment and to involve citizens in the course of events. In the absence of a stable hierarchy, the forms of governance that emerge will likely be "glocal", in the sense that they will permanently maintain interaction between global and local points of view and between collective intelligence and individual intelligences.

The word will be *self-governance* rather than governance: if there's anything left that resembles a government, its role will be less to select orientations or make decisions, than to ensure that the social organism remains in good health, i.e., able to choose orientations that work for the common good.

Political think tanks are multiplying and reflecting on the reforms needed to redress our socio-economies and on what could be a deepening of democracy. Some of these think tanks probably foreshadow important organs of a future societal democracy. Polls on voting intentions help political parties to cautiously open up to a people's society. Through these polls, voters begin to have some influence on party life.

A growth in awareness: the base, the ground level of society, wants to communicate directly.

During the early 2010s, "big coalitions" - national unions - were formed here and there. They corresponded both to some leaders' awareness of the seriousness of the situation, and to the weariness of citizens faced with the vanity of partisan fighting and the paralysis it induced.

Towards a participative democracy

In early 2014, 10 of the 18 countries in the Eurozone were governed by a coalition. Beyond the ideological cleavages, people spoke of governments of public welfare, independent of parties and the political class. The society of people in which an ideal of co-operation was developing started to influence political life in the countries of the North: Sweden, Denmark, Germany and England. France seemed to be one of the countries anchored in a right-left division and the preservation of bureaucratic and hierarchical structures. But in 2017, a disruption occurred: breaking with ideologies and parties, Emmanuel Macron combined right and left, and made them work more or less "together".

"En Marche", the movement that got Macron elected, was action oriented. On the basis of individual experiences, he fueled a collective emotion of together being able to influence the course of events. The desire for profound change was in everyone's mind. Where the movement seemed to make a big difference was in the very strong involvement of the society of ordinary people, in the search for deliberations evolving from the bottom up. This way of searching out new mechanisms for political adjustment corresponds quite well to the needs of metamorphosed people.

The success of the Macron campaign was at least partly due to the fact that it was in tune with the humanistic metamorphosis. Citizens prefer cooperation to conflict. Macron's electoral campaign was carried along by the ongoing metamorphosis, while his behavior as president is at odds with it. Looking at the evolution of European countries in the following chapters, we will see the current political obstacles to metamorphosis, the reactions of the people's society and the rise in seven countries of so-called "populist" governments that surf on the abandonment felt by people who no longer believe in representative democracy.

SOCIETAL COAGULATIONS, COLLECTIVE EMOTIONS AND THE ANGER OF THE PEOPLE

Bubbling collective emotions coagulate into demonstrations. These gatherings and explosions express the affirmation of a community, of an identity, and also an exasperation, a dissent, which could be pre-revolutionary. "Je suis Charlie" (I am Charlie) was a republican demonstration of collective identity. Spontaneous demonstrations of solidarity with the victims of the terrorist attack at the offices of Charlie Hebdo sprang up throughout France on January 8 and 9, 2015. An astonishing popular communion around republican values animated the country for several weeks. It was as if a scattered society of ordinary people and a divided political society found immense satisfaction in uniting and proclaiming their unity and strength.

Indignados, Podemos, and Occupy Wall Street are movements that have occupied city centers and town squares since spring 2011. Using their smartphones, amateur street reporters filmed the demonstrations and circulated the footage on their networks, sometimes to large audiences on TV channels. Active on social networks, the movements drew inspiration from the "Arab Spring", in particular the Tunisian and Egyptian revolutions, and from the important "Indignés" movement in Europe. On October 15, 2011 - five months after the initial Spanish manifestations of 15 May - hundreds of thousands across the world participated in a "Worldwide Day of

Indignation": demonstrations took place in London, Tel-Aviv, New York, Montreal, Tokyo, and Johannesburg.

In France during 2012-13, a powerful movement of popular opinion arose against the adoption of a law instituting homosexual marriage, known as "marriage for all". The demonstrators contested the legitimacy of the law voted by parliamentarians elected by universal suffrage some months earlier, and demanded a referendum. This was the intent of direct democracy.

The big winners of the Italian general elections in March 2018 depended on a motley crew of collaborators. A non-party, the 5 Star Movement led by comic actor Bepe Grillo, sought power through an alliance with an extreme right-wing party, La Liga, led by Matteo Salvini. The label *"directismo"* had emerged some years earlier in Italy to designate the search for direct democracy operating through the Internet.

The 5 Star Movement had a charismatic leader. The most symptomatic movements are those that are born and develop without a leader, without a definite ideology, and are nourished by shared emotions. In France, demonstrations against the tax burden are becoming more frequent, involving individuals and companies in difficulty - for example the "Bonnets rouges" (Red Bonnets) and the "Gilets Jaunes" (Yellow Vests).

The Gilets Jaunes, a movement that has shaken France in 2018 and 2019

The starting point for the movement was an increase in the price of fuel to facilitate the transition away from fossil fuels. The announcement resulted in severe distress among ordinary people struggling to make ends meet, and the feeling that the common good is no longer assured. These people are socio-perceptive: they sense that the ecosystem is no longer good for them. This is true particularly in rural areas or small towns neglected by land use planning in terms of transport, medical equipment, nurseries, schools, job opportunities, etc. Their inhabitants are totally dependent on the automobile in their daily lives. They are very diverse people who have often never attended a demonstration and have had little or no involvement in elections. Retirees, women in the home, farmers - they feel isolated, and have discovered with joy what the vitality and warmth of a social network can be, focusing on words such as "fraternity" and "solidarity". There was, originally, a good-natured, playful side to the Yellow Vest movement. It was based in a practical sense on the fact that in France every vehicle is required by law to carry a government-sponsored high-visibility yellow vest, to be worn in the event of an accident.

The special character of movements developing today around social networks is that there is no leader, no organization with which the public authorities can discuss. They do not want to be represented. We are in the complexity of "dissipative systems": self-regulation is or is not carried out, depending on each network member and on internal and external pressures, which can be considerable. There is a profound ambiguity in the various positions adopted: Yellow Vests may not be fundamentally against ecological management unless they really do not care about the environment, but they feel uncomfortable in their immediate lives and are looking for ways to cope on a daily basis. Linked to this acute collective socio-perception that the common good is no longer assured, the movement may, one way or another, last a very long time.

The Yellow Vests want to be heard; they want mayors and other forms of local organization to be listened to by central authorities. And when their disenchantment is crystallized on a person, their "indignation", manipulated by extremists, turns into anger that can be very destructive and dangerous for the balance of society. Dialogue seems difficult. Will it develop into a large national debate? Will such a debate be organized from the top down or, as the Yellow Vests wish, from the grassroots? We urgently need "catalysts for public action" in situations of extreme complexity. Can natural self-organizations – "hybrid collectives" uniting public bodies, intermediary bodies, unions, associations - be "facilitators of self-organization" in a complex system? In a system of manipulatable networks, short-term and long-term seem irreconcilable, and the antithesis of humanistic metamorphosis. But metamorphosis is also about turning crises into opportunities. It is the caterpillar that becomes a butterfly. What will the imaginal cells of the chrysalis do? Could the Yellow Vest movement, currently being co-opted by political extremists, be a chance for Emmanuel Macron to abandon technocratic expertise and get closer to the real lives of ordinary people by favoring public action through local soft power? You can't decide what will be the future.

The rise of populism, structural or groundless shift?

Living organisms are, as we have said, self-adjusting: they regenerate themselves constantly in interaction with their environment. It is therefore to be expected that a process of metamorphosis can bifurcate. We are at a junction where the metamorphosis of humanity can be hijacked to the benefit of political, financial, technological, religious or communitarian oligarchies. Optimistic or pessimistic future scenarios are before us. Fluctuations announcing possible bifurcations may prompt us to intervene to nurture or to divert them. At these tipping points, a chaotic future is conceivable.

State and corporate governance remains in place and in many cases continues to be unable to provide for the common good. A new class struggle seeks effective forms. Alliances are formed. Revolutions occur. Happy metamorphosis is postponed. We can thus foresee communitarian antagonisms continuing to develop in most European countries. Salafist terrorism reinforces anti-Muslim populism. Governments, whether right-wing, left-wing, or even coalition, cannot engage with the people's society and do not succeed in easing tensions. Coagulations multiply. Electoral patterns are overthrown. Political regimes collapse. More or less fascist authoritarian governments are temporarily established in some countries. This possible scenario, described a few years ago[48], is proving to be increasingly relevant in the Europe of 2018.

Populisms expressed through Brexit, the election of Trump, Catalan separatism, the Italian elections of 2018, are all the expression of the rejection of the traditional political system. Today a disenchanted people is turning to strong populist leaders, whether in the United States, China, Turkey, Hungary or elsewhere.

Perceptions of the major societal, economic and moral issues are expressed as feelings of loss of identity, loss of meaning, uncontrolled migration, unemployment, the impoverishment of entire sections of the population, the feeling of insecurity, imposed multiculturalism, religious extremisms financed by oil, terrorism that can arise at every street corner, "fake news", "slanderous information" broadcast by manipulated social networks, and, of course, climatic deterioration and health problems.

European governments have allowed suburban ghettos to develop where life is hard and relationships are tough. In a family that may be lack stability, young people do not always receive the tenderness that favors socialization. Some, failing at school, can barely read and have only a few

---

48. Les Carnets de la metamorphose, www.happymorphose.com, quarterly publication.

hundred words at their disposal. In a modern economy they are unlikely to find a stable job. Their reasoning ability is reduced and their emotional and relational intelligence is crude. Most did not have any religious environment in their family. They have stored up aggression and perhaps hatred of this society. They may lean towards crime or terrorism, and today very specifically towards jihadism.

In a context of extreme international tensions, many countries have developed nuclear weapons. Local conflicts have erupted. Migrations poison the atmosphere. Terrorism is proliferating. A warlike metamorphosis is curdling the humanist metamorphosis. It is easy to imagine processes that would affect the course of humanistic metamorphosis. Some would interrupt its progress and install a new authoritarian state civilization, leading to disorder or wars. The European Union as it has been constituted for more than half a century could break up and new groups formed.

Could the humanistic metamorphosis veer into a dead end leading to an oligarchic metamorphosis?

If Western financial circles or the American military-industrial complex, or hackers or the Chinese Communist Party, or members of the French administrative elite, or veteran transhumanists took control over Big Data and became skilled socio-perceptive manipulators, could they constitute a more or less hidden, sustainable ruling caste? The explosions of Western youth around 1968 crossed national and continental boundaries and spread like wildfire. They were not political revolutions, but societal and cultural revolts against an oppressive society: conventions, parents, teachers, authorities in everyday life. It turned out afterwards that they were weak signals announcing the sociocultural change of the following decades and the rise in power of ordinary people. Popular coagulation over the years 2010-2020 could herald an accelerated transition to another form of democracy, unless rising challenges thwart metamorphosis and give prominence to populism and authoritarian governments.

But the process of bottom-up humanistic metamorphosis is gathering considerable strength and allows us to hope that when we come to the crossroads, we will take the right turning.

How can we test new public policies that simplify administration and "bring territorial democracy to life?" A society of people sometimes feels that it exists as a united whole and shares a democratic life. Popular coagulations can strengthen this democracy, or block it through upheaval or co-optation. But in a chaotic world, islands of resistance settle in different places based on intuitive, empathic, socio-perceptive people, and on the strength of the networks of solidarity described above. These forces could reorient society towards a happy semi-metamorphosis, either "Confucian" (that is, organized from above as a gift from heaven and empathic); personalized to suit Western culture; or setting a radically new direction. "Societal democracies" based on empowerment, acceptance of responsibility and personal autonomy may be born out of disorder.

PATHS FOR THE FUTURE: WHAT LESSONS CAN WE LEARN?

Metamorphosis destabilizes our statist, hierarchical, bureaucratic governance. In Europe, since the Treaty of

Westphalia, states are sovereign, deemed to be masters at home. In the twentieth century, whether they are elected democratically or dictatorial, they govern from above, enact laws and regulations that apply to all and lead nations based on bureaucratic and hierarchical administrations. They thus remain in the continuity of most civilizations humanity has built since Sumer. During the "Glorious Thirty" years following World War II, states increased their power by taking responsibility for the people's happiness, perfecting their bureaucratic organization, and relying on the orchestration of ideologies and the manipulation of citizens who were still easy to influence. But they were caught off guard by the process of metamorphosis. As people became more personally independent, autonomous and vital, connected with each other more freely and horizontally in an infinitely more complex society, the hierarchical, bureaucratic, and manipulative character of governance not only became exasperating, but a factor of turbulence and inefficiency.

Need for catalysts of public action

To exert influence or leadership over a system, one must sense its dynamics and trends and intervene in a timely manner to generate, collect, and catalyze the intended responses.

In these first decades of the twenty-first century, our governments are struggling to govern. They no longer engage the sources of dynamism, innovation, growth, and employment. The bureaucratic state, instead of favoring positive attitudes to life, restrains innovation, provokes sterilization, prevents vital encounters from occurring at the base and the formation of synergies which would give birth to companies or innovative networks. We could give many examples[49].

A society seeking not so much competition and performance as fulfillment and optimization expects a responsible politician to know how to ensure that the organism in his charge adopts approaches that optimize its development and that of its ecosystems.

Metamorphosis runs up against mental models that are centuries old. This change, however, is facilitated by states' loss of capacity to intervene. Indeed, European states have abandoned part of their sovereignty for the benefit of the European Union. Globalization of the economy and the planet-wide nature of ecological challenges facing them have reduced their ability to maneuver against international markets and companies. Moreover, the weight of their public debt is forcing Western governments to cut back on state spending, further reducing their fields of action. Other ways must be found.

Awareness is spreading that decentralization facilitates the evolution of governance and participation. It is also realized that subsidiarity - a tool of decentralization within the framework of a globally hierarchical organization - can be replaced by egalitarian State/region dialogue and cooperation. Let us consider Switzerland. Locally, the talk is of self-governance rather than governance: if there is something like a government, its role will be less to choose directions or to make decisions than to keep the body healthy: that is, in a state to choose orientations that conform to the common good.

---

[49] Jo Spiegel:, *Et si on prenait enfin les électeurs au sérieux* (What if we finally took the voters seriously?), Temps Présent, 2017.

The renewal of generations, the risks of revolution, will facilitate the paradigm shift. But slowly. Awareness will develop. Political leaders have already realized that they have to change themselves in order to change society.

From a tutelary state to an attentive society

Seventy years ago, after the war, Europe drew inspiration from the examples of Sweden and England and from the American New Deal, to establish a radically new social contract, suited to Europe's society and economy at that time. The welfare state, a source of security, made a significant contribution to the remarkable economic and social progress of the third quarter of the twentieth century, and the installation of metamorphosis. This uniform contract was well adapted to the organized mass society characteristic of Western civilization at the stage it had then reached. It made the state the protector of all.

Today, most European countries have begun to unravel this all-embracing contract. The intensification of global competition makes it economically unsustainable in the absence of full employment. Its generalized and bureaucratic nature makes it counterproductive in a complex, varied, and changing society.

The new society of people, with its networks, its socio-systems and its collectives, is attentive to the optimization of its operations.

Fraternal social security

The new society would focus on monitoring individuals on a case-by-case basis: relying on a high degree of decentralization and the immense potential of IT, individuals could be assisted according to their specific needs, allowing them to make the most of their potential.

New collectivities and networks of family and friends would intervene to help the unemployed, sick, handicapped, and isolated to find the resources to surmount life's setbacks. The metamorphosis in progress is seeing a multiplication of psychologically well-equipped people whose vitality is galvanized by challenges such as unemployment, illness, divorce, unwanted pregnancy, bereavement and others. Talent remains undeveloped as it is difficult to mitigate disastrous educational pathways.

Optimization and fulfillment

The society of people who self-organize and take care of themselves looks for optimization and fulfillment. Its networks and hybrid collectives welcome life-enhancing innovations and seek to remedy established pathologies and perverse innovations. Individuals, networks, and organizations improvise warning signals. In this way, a self-regulating system develops, incorporating both prevention and cure. Our societies will have to equip themselves with the means to monitor their state of health, and develop a combination of socio-analysis and governance - a sort of societal medicine.

One of the major characteristics of the current metamorphosis is that it creates very favorable conditions for mobilizing individual. It ensures a better use by society of the available human potential. Some collectives are committed to ensuring the preservation and development of this equality of opportunity. Others seek to adapt teaching in order to reduce those aspects related to overdeveloped rationalism. Yet others want to take full advantage of the possibilities for personal customization brought by new information technologies.

Education and training are becoming dominant concerns that will attract growing investment and increasing staff, such that the educational pathway of young children - in the family, in society, and in school - does not lock them into a predetermined professional and social destiny. The goal is to enable children to become adaptable personalities capable of operating in the complexities of the modern world, and to ensure that educational supplements are provided in a timely manner to facilitate career reorientation or to correct past deficiencies. Tailor-made education must be adapted, on a case-by-case basis, to the profile and potentials of each.

POSSIBLE EVOLUTION TOWARDS A PARTICIPATIVE SOCIETAL DEMOCRACY: THE ROLE OF COLLECTIVE INTELLIGENCE

By feeling our way, by letting projects develop from the bottom up, conceived regionally and in the "new hybrid collectives", could we move towards another form of democracy, locally rooted, in line with the humanist metamorphosis?[50] This would require that leaders agree to follow the currents of humanist metamorphosis. But in the context of a representative democracy, they do not know how to manage the dilemma of necessary reforms coupled with attentive governance. How is one to be a catalyst for the emerging impulses of a living society, while maintaining coherence, co-creating a shared vision for society, and taking into account local initiatives? How is one to enable the growth of collective intelligence

---
50. Jo Spiegel, *op. cit.*

that must not be confused with public opinion which is too often manipulated by traditional media or state organizations?

The words to express this challenge cut both ways: growing awareness, developing empowerment, trial and error, tentative strategies, "do-it-yourself" society, letting people organize themselves in specific projects, lighten the weight of bureaucratic control, without forgetting the time factor. Is it possible? For a better understanding of the need and desire for this growth, these changes, we must take a look at the planet-wide challenges facing us, and the global extension of the humanist metamorphosis.

Chapter 10.
Towards a planet-wide metamorphosis: East and West

Different parts of the world have always metamorphosed in their own way and at their own speed. Today, metamorphosis concerns the entire planet and the human species as a whole.

Planet Earth - mineral, vegetable and animal - has become a human planet. Its regions are more and more intensely connected. The Internet allows us to interact in real time with our colleague, our friend or our enemy on the opposite side of the world. We can operate a drone thousands of kilometers from our command post.

Since the late 1980s, under the combined influences of industrialization, market liberalization, the collapse of the Soviet system and of several dictatorships, misery has dramatically declined worldwide and, at the same time, a middle class of consumers has developed in Russia, China, India, and several Southeast Asian and Latin American countries. Between 1990 and 2015, one billion people escaped the most extreme poverty, that is to say, a situation where the main concern is foraging for survival. They see the possibility of escaping misery soon. They understand that they have the right to hope for a better life. They dream, some make plans, others move. They are

Part III. A great bifurcation

setting on a road that will make them capable of taking initiative.

The geopolitical structure of the planet is changing. After the collapse of the Soviet bloc, it did not seem out of the question that history had made a lasting commitment to a unipolar planet dominated by the United States - policemen of the world - who would impose their way of life and their values everywhere. But from the ruses of History another path has emerged. Globalization, desired and driven by the United States, has freed worldwide flows of information, goods, capital, technology, and tasks. It has quickly changed the face of the world, and initiated a redistribution of power centers on the planet. The economies of Europe and Japan are stagnating. India is progressing. Russia is gradually waking up. Growth is spreading across much of the developing world, including Africa. But, above all, China has made a tremendous leap forward at a speed that has never been matched. The United States remains the leading power; however, in the complexities of the twenty-first century, even overwhelming power cannot impose its law.

The global social fabric is becoming very complex. Powers of different and fluctuating forms interact, cooperate, compete, sometimes threaten each other or fight. NGOs, multinationals, mafias, terrorist networks, etc., multiply. Nation states have lost their sovereignty. Together, they now form an inter-communicating network. Their leaders call, visit easily. National identities remain but are less distinct. The regions of the world are connected to each other by monetary, economic, and human flows. Even small companies have the whole world for their market and as competition. Our economies have reached a planetary level of interdependence. In every country and region, bank failures, bankruptcies, and unemployment rates depend on what happens elsewhere and have repercussions elsewhere.

Young rebels from Tahrir Square in Cairo communicated with Western bloggers and hackers. Members of immigrant diasporas in Europe or North America can talk and see their family or friends back home for free via Skype, Whatsapp or Facetime. The society of people is tending towards a global presence, but with an industrial development which in its present forms is not sustainable.

THE CHALLENGES ARE PLANET-WIDE

The ecological threat

COP 21 was a crucial moment in the coupling of metamorphosis with the future of the planet. During the twentieth century, ecologist parties have not managed to exercise significant influence on managements of large companies or most governments. However, since the beginning of the twenty-first century, a collective awareness of climate change and the associated ecological danger has emerged. For the first time, COP 21 in Paris did not just involve states but opened up to the presence and effective participation of the society of people and its new organizational life-forms. Collective governance has begun to metamorphose, growing out of hyper-complex networks involving administrations, governments, civil society, and the society of ordinary people.

After long months of preparation based on openness, the process that involved actors from 195 countries in the protection of the planet was unique in its kind in its level of listening, dialogue, participation, and projects.

Even if all the expected effects are not yet there, even if Donald Trump wants to limit the effects, it is an exceptional step that will be remembered and probably repeated. This is undoubtedly one of the first high-profile manifestations of a coupling between societal metamorphosis and awareness of a major global issue - in this case climate change - which will reinforce each other. France's environmental round table was an initial step in this direction but on a national scale.

Nuclear and biological weapons

These sophisticated weapons are extremely dangerous and have the potential to decimate our populations or even destroy the planet. Nation states no longer have the control or monopoly of violence. The peoples of the Earth are now challenged to manage and regulate the geopolitics of the planet.

Steering socio-economic development

In the West, we have not managed the development of our economies wisely. Our incompetence has allowed for inequalities leading to social unrest, revolutions, wars, and economic and financial crises. Sometimes the situation is restored; sometimes the crisis leaves behind a fractured society. Earth's inhabitants see each other, everywhere - even in the remotest places. The poor see the rich, not only in their own country, but also elsewhere on the planet. Those who lack water see those who waste it. Those who feel excluded from modernity envy those who enjoy it. Humanity faces the challenge of regulating its development.

THE EURO-AMERICAN CIVILIZATION HAS RUBBED OFF ON THE WORLD

The images of Western life conveyed by cinema, television and travel have aroused desire more than rejection. Europe has given the world the tools to transform personalities, modes of existence, and relationships, such as capitalism, representative democracy and feminism. Among the most important forces of change are Marxism, birth control, the destruction of ancient bearers of meaning such as God, the Nation, the working class, or Progress. Developing countries import industrialization and consumption; within the emerging middle class, these imports bring about the transformation of personalities, mentalities, the social fabric and social control which, although not identical to the experiences of Europe and America, closely resemble them. They thus engage in the humanist metamorphosis they help to guide. The metamorphosis becomes a co-production of several ancient civilizations leading to a new planetary civilization. We are moving away from tribal, rural, and mass society. As in Europe in the 1950s and 1960s, the presence of desirable products and more or less accessible prestige brands awakens envy and triggers the imitation of neighbors. Confronted with choices, these new consumers watch what others do and wonder about their own emerging desires. They come into contact with their sensations, their emotions, their impulses; they individualize themselves, emerge from the masses, and escape from old frames of reference. They acquire a little autonomy. As in the West, the impact on everyday behavior - especially among women - is evident.

Unlike what has happened in the West, however, behaviors are emerging which defend against the captivating motivations for personal expression and accomplishment, leading people question their meaning and to take a critical distance from the race for consumption.

In Russia, a new hedonistic and consumptive voracity, typical of the European modernity of the 1950s and 1960s, coexists with profound elements in phase with metamorphosis: practice of personal fulfillment, spirituality, search for meaning, love of human relations, acute awareness of the limited place of man in nature. Is there another underlying type of metamorphosis in Russia? In China, there is the same concurrent development of an explosive race for consumption and real quests for autonomy and meaning. Latent human potentials are actualized; people become more aware of themselves and savvier, more concerned about the meaning of their lives, less easy to manipulate. Socio-political conditioning is easing: working communities and neighborhood communities that allowed the authorities and the party to closely monitor the lives of men and women are seeing their leadership roles reduced.

Metamorphosis does not necessarily proceed in the same sequence of phases as in the West. New entrants skip steps yet arrive at the same kinds of awareness as in the West, faster or by different paths.

Women are engines of socio-cultural evolution. The World Development Indicators of the World Bank show that in developing countries the balance of power is slowly but steadily improving for women. More and more women in these areas are becoming literate and attending secondary and higher education. They impose a decline in fertility. With the help of the media the liberation of women is reaching the whole planet, not only in the Indo-Chinese-Japanese world, but also in the Arab world. Women everywhere are transmitting socio-cultural change that individualizes, personalizes, and destroys hidebound authority.

Everywhere, in a growing portion of the population, love is becoming a value and sexual morals are relaxing. More and more couples meet online or through friends. Divorces are becoming more common.

The process of metamorphosis that was once a Western phenomenon is tending to become polycultural. Westerners will have to remain alert to new dynamics that may emerge in other parts of the world.

WESTERN AND CHINESE CIVILIZATIONS

The central roots and paradigms of traditional Chinese and Western civilizations seem to be opposed, but their rapprochement during the twentieth century may prepare them to engage in metamorphosis together.

Theology emerged in the West, while China developed manticology - phenomena beyond the visible. Growing out of of shamanism, manticology does not see the supernatural as incarnated in divine entities, but as the invisible double of the visible natural world, influencing the latter by a mysterious magical force which the shaman can access and on which he can possibly act. In all cultures men have tried to predict and influence the future. Chinese culture accepted complexity and was thus opposed to traditional Western culture that focused on simplification. The Yi King or Book of Changes is a system of binary signs used to anticipate changes. Starting from an opposition-complementarity, the yin and yang principles subdivide this duality in a systematic way and can include all the possible transformations of the states of the world. Chinese and Greek thought are not opposed. European culture was built on the debate between Parmenides (permanence) and Heraclitus (change). During the twentieth century, Chinese culture came closer to the West by absorbing rational thought, scientific thought, and Marxism. It assimilated the notions of simplification, analysis, causes, competition, planning, maximization, creation, truth.

Concurrently, European civilization, driven by metamorphosis, opened up to complexity. The evolution of everyday experiences as well as scientific developments propelled the paradigm of complexity and notions such as system, process, emergence, sequence of sequences, etc., and brought us closer to Chinese thought. At the same time, Europe and America, in search of meaning, became interested in Far Eastern spiritualities: yoga, Buddhism, Tao. This double movement of Chinese and European civilizations towards each other, and their common focus on complexity and systems, reinforces the hypothesis that metamorphosis can be global.

Governance systems could adapt to metamorphosis

The Chinese empire was structured around larger networks than the administrative partitions of a nation. The representative and partisan democracy practiced in the West was remarkably effective during the years following World War II, but is now out of step with metamorphosis, its efficiency and popular support diminished. Likewise, after the disasters of Mao's Great Leap Forward and the Cultural Revolution, China's one-party enlightened dictatorship has been very successful: it has driven the country's socio-economic development over the last 30 years with great success. But it is also causing frustrations, stresses, and vigorous challenges in a population where individual autonomy and social networks are growing. And, of course, in China modes of governance and management are slow to adapt to the metamorphosis of a people's society.

A powerful dictatorship is faced with 800 million Internet users, the collective expression of the people. The Chinese Internet is accelerating the formation of networks, mobility, and temporary coagulation, and is breeding new hybrid collectives. Propaganda and regimentation could lose their effectiveness. The existence and vitality of these Internet users and their links has probably already forced Chinese governance to evolve. Fundamentally dictatorial, the central power strives to control public opinion, putting dissidents in prison and censoring discussions on the Internet. At the same time, it is aware of protest movements and changes in sensitivities, and could possibly take them into account in an attempt to implement skillful piloting.

China: between tradition and modernity

In their analysis of Chinese society, Michel Aglietta and Guo Bai insist on "the mixture of tradition and modernity present in Chinese culture, which makes it possible to understand the resilience of social institutions"[51]. The social structure of imperial China was not very different from that of today's China. A ruling group (bureaucracy of highly literate, hand-picked officials, closely dependent on the Emperor's absolute central authority) faces a large population that forms a dense web of overlapping social relations. The bureaucracy is the transmission belt between the

---

51. Michel Aglietta and Guo Bai, *La Voie Chinoise : Capitalisme et Empire*, Odile Jacob, 2012, p. 17.

people and the central power and ensures the well-being of the population. This well-being legitimized the bureaucracy and the Emperor's Heavenly Mandate, just as it legitimizes the Party today.

There were and are few intermediary groups (aristocratic families, churches, cities, parties, etc.) to counterbalance the state; however, there were and still are organized solidary collectives. For example, in villages, public officials are often subject to informal rules and unwritten standards that improve the production of the common good[52].

The authors believe that today the Party is fully aware of the need to renew its membership if it wants to succeed in the new phase of reform that should lead the country towards economic sustainability. This renewal has been going on since the year 2000: civil servants are now younger and better trained than before, more attentive to the needs of the people, more socio-perceptive.

Aglietta and Guo Bai note that one of the strengths of the Chinese state system is its capacity to adapt to a diversity of situations. Communist China is not fixed on a particular ideology of right or left, but tries to maintain its position constantly through a trial and error strategy that aims to produce common good in both the short and long term. It may be that the history of the twenty-first century will show that, provided that the bureaucracy and the Party find the means to remain closely and permanently adjusted to the well-being of a people's society, this type of structure can lead to "society-as-a-brain" and a Chinese-style societal democracy.

Harvard professor Tu Weiming has been drawing attention for several years to the revival of Confucianism

---

52. Lily L. Tsai, Accountability Without Democracy: Solidarity Groups and Public Goods Provision in Rural China, Cambridge University Press, 2007.

among scholars and intellectuals in China and throughout Southeast Asia. Scholars from the China's People's Party[53] are celebrating the "Confucianization" of the Communist Party, advocating a Confucianist policy and a government following Confucian virtues of humanity. The resurgence of Confucianism seems to have arisen from the reaction of the society of people traumatized by the destabilization induced by very rapid growth, corruption and the proliferation of mafia systems, a reaction welcomed and instrumentalized by both party and government.

Confucianism is centered on civility, transmitted through rites whose observance ensures interiorization (what is appropriate, well-mannered, is transformed into fundamental honesty). This civility nourishes the smooth liaison of interpersonal and social relations and the search for harmony with the cosmic organization of nature, functioning organically according to the dynamism of yin and yang, the five elements and the four seasons. It seems that the Beijing authorities and the Communist Party, especially its young people, are encouraging this movement. Confucianism is a form of wisdom that puts man, the harmony of society, and good governance at the center of its concerns. A scenario can be glimpsed of an original process of metamorphosis developed from the Chinese tradition.

Confucianism could open up progressive and humanistic perspectives for political reform in China and elsewhere. Confucian reformers are in favor of greater freedom of expression. Different paths to the political future are open.

However, the current stiffening of the Chinese political system does not go in this direction. This is the ambiguity

---
53. such as Jiang Qing or Kang Xiaoguang.

of the president-as-emperor policy. Control of Chinese citizens is being strongly intensified; peaceful religious cohabitation is threatened. The great "One Belt, One Road Initiative" for the "New East-West Silk Roads" is burdened by uncertainties: is it an indispensable link between two old civilizations, or an instrument of power, defense and territorial conquest aimed at Asia, Africa, and Europe?

AMERICAN AND EUROPEAN UNCERTAINTIES

Europe and the United States together were initiators and pilots of humanistic metamorphosis.

The United States accelerated the process, even caricatured it. Inventing hippies and the New Age in California in the 1960s, obsessed with personal expression in the 1970s, pioneering social network in the 1990s, the United States are a cultural innovator. Its ability to scale up technical innovations crucial to metamorphosis, such as mass production, mass marketing and the Internet gave it planet-wide influence.

However the United States has steadfastly maintained its resistance to such socio-cultural change, embodied in a segment of conservatives very attached to old Christian values and beliefs, and traditional conceptions of the family and hierarchy. A very powerful ruling class and political establishment are under the influence of economic and financial lobbies, the military-industrial complex and the power of money. They block possible advances towards a societal democracy, a sustainable socio-economy, the fight against the increasing inequality, or the struggle for solidarity and equality of opportunity. They sin by excess of liberalism.

Governance introduced by metamorphosis would combine laissez-faire with vigilance. It would tend to allow development of spontaneous popular movements which are often beneficial, but with careful monitoring to identify possible dangerous deviations.

Conversely, US governance has consistently stated a preference for uncontrolled laissez-faire. Hard science - heir to hypertrophied nineteenth century rationalism - which refuses to make room for the emotional and spiritual dimensions of the human experience, is developing more easily in the United States and especially in California than in Europe, for example in the form of transhumanist experimentation. The financialization of capitalism invented and promoted by America and transmitted to Europe disrupted and slowed metamorphosis. Even more than Europe, the United States is currently in poor political health. Representative democracy works badly there.

The political system is jammed. Special interests weigh heavily on political activity. Governance makes inappropriate decisions. Inequalities are widening. The 2008 crisis affected American society very deeply. Part of the population is condemned to a life of precarity.

A huge debt has been accumulated. Americans share a culture of violence and a taste for weapons. The United States remains nationalist, domineering and imperious if not imperialistic. Military spending is massive - greater than that of the rest of the world together. In a world that is becoming multipolar, the US will probably remain the greatest economic and military power for quite a long time. With its development of "special forces" units, armed drones and cyber-attacks, the US is embarking on a global, non-territorial strategy to destroy enemy forces, whether state or non-state. America considers itself exceptional, and refuses to comply with various international conventions. In the face of terrorism, it has felt entitled to practice torture, illegal imprisonment, and widespread espionage.

Since September 11, 2001 and the vote of the Patriot Act, American governments have freed themselves from respect for its own constitutional rights. These practices are awakening whistleblowers (such as Bradley Manning or Edward Snowden). The courts condemn them, but their convictions arouse protests. The role we may expect the United States to play may take a number of different directions. It cannot afford to be as ubiquitous as in previous decades, and is now tending to refocus on vital interests, with implications for the rest of the world and especially for their European allies, who are becoming more partners or competitors than allies.

In this second decade of the twenty-first century, major ecological, geopolitical and biological tragedies threaten the human species. They will be better managed and the resilience of affected societies will stronger, the more the process of metamorphosis is advanced. Political and economic life and their management structures will be better adapted to the society of the people. It is vital to hasten and facilitate the birth of our metamorphosis.

The CIA's scenarios in the face of metamorphosis

The American National Intelligence Council, the observation and economic intelligence arm of the CIA, conducts a broad prospective study every four years on the possible future of the planet. In 2013, it envisioned four scenarios, reduced in 2017 to three. They show how the American establishment sees the global future over the next 15 years, with its hesitations, fears and preferences. In the last two studies, one of the scenarios embodies a version of metamorphosis as we understand it.

In 2017, this third scenario - entitled "Communities" - explores the issues raised by upcoming challenges in the field of economics and governance that, by putting governments to the test, will create space for local communities and private actors, questioning our certainties about future modes of government. This scenario shows that governments will need to encourage public-private partnerships with a variety of actors, NGOs, and civil society associations, in order to respond to emerging issues. Businesses and charities in particular could be increasingly associated with government work in areas of research, education, health, and information.

The progress of this last scenario over time has attracted our attention because it deals with geopolitical and economic dangers, and the temptations of territorial isolation which cause so much anguish today.

A scenario of soft power seen in terms of metamorphosis

Influence networks become more creative than direct power.

Under the influence of the military-industrial complex and financial lobbies, and the weight of conservative and traditionalist circles, the United States remains stuck in a representative presidential democracy and a hyperfinancial and short-termist capitalism that does not reduce inequalities. Governance can no longer respond to the country's social challenges or cope with expenditures for

Part III. A great bifurcation

the general interest. Today the United States is struggling to live up to its image and its global ambitions. A section of the populace feels badly governed and is reluctant to support the government.

China has seen its economic growth continue although at a slower rate. The Communist Party, purged of corruption, has become resolutely Confucian. The government is strengthening its authority and continues to maneuver around social networks to avoid major unrest. Be that as it may, followers of Buddhist, Taoist and Christian movements are increasing. Interstate tensions in the Pacific Ocean remain strong.

In Europe, frequent political coagulations and the spectacular successes of populist parties in various elections in 2014, 2015 and 2018 have sounded the alarm and stimulated innovation. Here and there, right-wing and left-wing governing parties see their constituents and activists drop away, shaking them to their foundations. Unexpected alliances are forming. The discredit of professional politicians is reaching new summits. The basic personality and physiology of European societies undergoing metamorphosis are increasingly allergic to representative and partisan democracy, which is also discredited and increasingly appears as a formal democratic mask hiding an oligarchic elite. Faced with the migration crisis, the European Union is shaking but has not broken. What is going on?

European society is now more advanced on the path of humanist metamorphosis than the United States or China, but the EU is in danger of breaking up, and its global role seems to have diminished. Is it conceivable that a non-state scenario could emerge without major upheavals, in which another Europe could occupy the position of conductor of the orchestra, a temporary catalyst for humanist metamorphosis?

Chapter 11.
And what about Europe?

In an EU that is falling between two stools, Europeans hesitate between their attachment to their country and a desire to ensure the existence of Europe as a political entity, participating peacefully in international affairs. From decade to decade, stumbling from alliances to conflicts, from progress to withdrawals, Europe is feeling its way forward. It is both in phase and in opposition to metamorphosis. In phase, the smaller powers of each of the 27 countries interact, offsetting each other and weighing on the decision-making process according to the circumstances. And they allow national, regional and sectoral players to continue to exist. This bureaucratic system of governance, which today is "complicated" and inefficient, could tomorrow perhaps become "complex" and alive. Such a network of actors - none of whom is sovereign - permanently dominating the others, is compatible with the process of metamorphosis and will contribute to the establishment of a societal, post-statist democracy in Europe - on the condition that it succeeds in connecting closely with the lived experiences of ordinary people and the socio-economy. By contrast, the disordered interactions of these participants do not lead to shared visions of the future or to effective strategies for integrating Europe into the global socio-economy. This inefficiency raises waves of protest among the peoples of Europe.

ANOTHER EUROPE IS PUTTING ITSELF TOGETHER

People feel it and accuse the European Union of not protecting them against competition from developing countries or from the influx of migrants. In a referendum, the United Kingdom voted against remaining in the European Union: Brexit. And European power has a tendency to standardize national and regional differences rather being enriched by them. It thus goes against the grain of our metamorphosis.

Can the EU cooperate with new collectives and companies from various European countries, or with different regions of member nations, to tackle the concrete problems facing Europe? Major challenges include pollution, energy savings, reduction of unemployment, exports outside Europe, control of migration, integration of Muslim populations, and the means of creating of an attentive society? The European Union, to the extent that it is post-national and post-state, that it relies on diversity in unity, that it is a living development rather than a planned construction, could embody the metamorphosis. European political power as it is now organized is a system that has its own logic. It is inefficient but resists change because it maintains the career benefits of the players involved. It evolves only slowly under the influence of the process of metamorphosis. On the other hand, the society of people is changing rapidly with the emergence of new generations of hybrid collectives. The gap between political power and living society is widening. This is generating turbulence in multiple areas: disenchantment and populism; reduced purchasing power; invasive unemployment; young people permanently unemployed; increasing numbers of people evicted from their homes; loss of social benefits and disintegration of the welfare state; postponed retirement; work and life in companies become harder; loss of company meaning; invasion of the economy by finance; abandonment of workers' conquests; growing inequalities; "My children may have a worse life than mine".

Two approaches are particularly frequent.

- Part of the population, more or less in phase with metamorphosis, distance themselves from politics and seek to flourish and find meaning in their personal lives. These people feel pretty well equipped to deal with difficulties. Many are involved in new collectives where they find social inclusion and meaning. Many are immersed in social networks. They are not militant; they condemn government parties, and often abstain from elections; however, they are may be mobilized, as we have seen, by protest movements, provided they feel intimate emotional resonance with them.
- Others would like to return to the past, to the way things were before, so as not to suffer any longer. This past is sometimes "the Revolution", as it was dreamed of a few decades ago. This vision is most often of the country, the Nation prior to Europe, before modernity, before the multicultural invasion. These nostalgics feed the populist movements. Coming from the far right and sometimes from the extreme left, these parties have been developing since the mid-1990s. They are nationalist, xenophobic, protectionist, anti-Muslim, opposed to the construction of Europe; they dream of a return to the earlier situation. Populism affects virtually every country in Europe.

The process of metamorphosis is robust. In Europe, the linkages between people's behavior, their networks, new collectives, and some political leaders continue to fuel the metamorphosis. Hybrid collectives continue to multiply, to connect with each other and to become aware of their strength.

An experimental socio-economy

An increasing number of companies and public actors are involved - in collaboration with offshoots from the society of ordinary people - in hybrid ecosystems that seek to fill deficits of common good such as unemployment, school failure, communitarian conflicts and others. A new stage of socio-technological coupling is thus beginning, which could profoundly transform the socio-economy and pave the way for approaches to societal participatory democracy.

Values, technologies, fields of competition, rules of the game, scientific research: all are in radical transformation. A new wave of innovative start-ups is forming. Perhaps more particularly in Europe, the idea is spreading that finance must serve the economy, and the economy must serve society and the global ecology. Managers who were focused on their very short-term financial results are again becoming interested in the medium and long term.

How is consumption changing? What products should be offered, what know-how must be mastered in order to find promising markets in ten years' time? What technological revolutions must be effected? What cultural revolutions are needed to adapt the company to the requirements of young employees? The society of people is aware of the seriousness of climate change and the need to radically review our energy behaviors.

A new branch of the economy, a kind of experimental socio-economy, is developing which is revolutionizing development aid.

Changes in the educational pathways of young people could spark more or less major bifurcations in one direction or the other.

Europe, a laboratory for societal democracy

In a hyper-complex world, Europe is a laboratory for societal democracy because, fundamentally, it is based on the acceptance of diversity: there is no single "European way of life".

This new European societal democracy is flourishing, both in research and in fact. From north to south, we observe them it locally, including in the "liberated administrations" in French towns such as Kingersheim; in Stockholm[54], Riace de Calabria[55], Greece[56], and elsewhere. It is urgent to launch research on these local projects which, thanks to digital communications, can connect with each other and become transnational.

The Europe of networks, based on concrete projects

It is a Europe that is not technocratic but alive: the Europe of new hybrid collectives.

These projects are evolving "on the ground." Those who were considered "administered", then "clients of

---

54. Fondation Ekskaret
55. "Un paese di Calabria", documentary film on the integration of migrants
56. Actions in the field by World Human Forum and reception of migrants, Place Victoria, Athens

the administration", have now become citizens and co-actors. We know the major projects in progress: Airbus, Erasmus, Artificial Intelligence, "Chimie Douce". But others are emerging and can continue to emerge: Erasmus apprenticeships (work-study contracts; professional accreditation) hosted in European companies; networks of universities focused on the creation of companies, etc.

The hybrid collectives - the "new hybrids" - are an expression of this new involvement of the people in their democracy. There is a rise in collective intelligence ("extelligence", or shared intelligence outside your own skull), is intuitively perceived by harvesting the "weak signals" of metamorphosis.

Within this political void, several European countries are seeing think tanks increasingly becoming do tanks of a fairly new kind. They operate on a regional, national, European or even global scale. In harmony with collective feeling, they openly display their independence from political parties, which they consider responsible for the crisis, and avoid situating themselves on the right/left continuum.

These citizen initiatives lead to serious experiments in new forms of participatory democracy, new forms of intelligent political networks. In the field, they research deficits in the common good and societal unrest.

They are triggers and then amplifiers of a fairly new public debate that, in a decade, will cover intra- and inter-partisan debate and accompany change in the political climate.

When these do tanks debate the urgent problems facing Europe - such as the choice of economic and industrial policy, the organization of education, the influx of migrants on the Mediterranean rim, Euroscepticism or

Islamist terrorism - they approach them in a radically new way, independent of ideological prejudice. They seek to ensure that the debate leads to solutions that can be tested and foster consensus. The climate shifts from "my solution is right" to "let's find the right solution together", following Gandhi's expression, "Everything you do for me without me, you do against me".

Since 2010, certain associations and citizen networks have worked to connect themselves and to map new European hybrid collectives and agents of change of all kinds. As a result, in a few years these groups and individuals have become aware of their extensive variety and importance. They have become interconnected, and a growing proportion of them have understood that they are the bearers of a fabulous transformation, and that they are essential elements of a true living society, the antithesis of a society of ruling castes overtaken by history. They feel invested with the power to change society, and show it by developing a dominant influence on the web.

Many public actors - especially municipal or regional bodies and most companies - have become aware of this evolution and have sought to establish partnerships with new groupings from the society of people, exploring tentative forms of hybrid power. From the joint influence of do tanks and the hybrid collectives have emerged a number of informal groupings. Towns are a particularly rich learning ground for these new organizations.

Part III. A great bifurcation

EUROPEANS-AS-A-BRAIN

Three poles have progressively become clearer and have become centers of political orientation, inspiring the governance of regions, companies, and the European Union as a whole.

- The first is concerned with the societal: it brings together people, networks, and organizations that take care of the vitality, the development, and the optimization of people as a society. The Swedes are launching research on societal democracy[57], which other European countries will join.
- The second pole focuses on planetary ecology, climate protection and energy transition.
- The third pole oversees the preservation of the human spirit.

All three are concerned with collective intelligence. Representatives of these poles have their place in political and economic governance bodies. They embody the consciousness of the system and influence the emergence of consensus about the common good and urgent repairs.

Will the media turn away from political theater, and look more closely at the society of people, at current movements and tendencies? The spotlight is less focused on electoral competition and much more on changes in substance and on future preparations for the common good. Metamorphosis, biomimicry, alliance with nature, fulfillment, frugality, and energy transition are becoming motivating themes. Metamorphosis could become society's driving myth, as in other times were Progress or Modernity or Personal Expression.

---

57. Fondation Ekskäret

"Europeans-as-a-brain" was, following our way of thinking, the theme in May 2018 of a major conference in Milan on sustainable development[58], "to make Europe a world leader in sustainable development where networks, partnerships and initiatives contributing to the implementation of such objectives work together to address the need to move forward, including a new social contract. The "Europeans-as-a-brain" initiative was to begin as an initial European ecosystem of organizations and processes".

Observatories of the living society

Set up here and there alongside the big pre-existing statistical structures, they provide a deeper, permanent socioanalysis of our evolving societies. They are on the lookout for emerging trends and weak signals of inflection of shaping trends. They observe changes in well-being and malaise in different segments of the population. They nourish the socio-perception of society by itself. They are focused on various areas of sociological and economic research and on Big Data, funded by administrations, foundations, business groups, universities, and think tanks, or by their clients. Their work is disseminated and feeds the strategic thinking of companies, start-ups, associations of all kinds, think tanks and networks preparing major policy choices. In competition with each other, they seek to develop methods of evaluating popular acquiescence and rejection. They perfect and refine their tools and research methods and are becoming essential instruments for dispersed, wise and sensitive steering of societies and hyper-complex economies.

---

58. www.epe.be, www.raymondvanermen.org

IS A EUROPEAN "SOFT POWER" SCENARIO FEASIBLE?

During the troubled period of 2010-2020, pessimism prevails. Disasters seem imminent. Europe hesitates about itself. Democracy is no longer a source of confidence. European nations are searching for their identity, threatened by waves of immigrants. A resurgence of religious fundamentalism threatens. Dangerous scientific and technical research is increasing. Governments do not respond to imminent climate disasters. Warlike tensions re-awake. Europe is faltering.

This dark climate has alerted the spirit of humanist metamorphosis. The dialogue between rational and spiritual intelligences had deepened. We have tried to understand what eluded us, and it had resulted in some discoveries. Humanist neo-spiritualist movements, centered on the spirit of Man, have come together to think and act in union. They have begun to dialogue with leading scientific circles and with monotheistic religions, including emerging Islam in Europe. Scientific and spiritual coordination and ethics committees, bearers of wisdom, have quickly gained influence, especially in establishing regulations to control hyper-capitalism and transhumanist operations.

The whistleblowers, too, have organized themselves. They take care to maintain the independence of a living society, the singularity of the human being, and aim to maintain the balance between collective and individual optimizations. Is the soft power scenario developed below possible, or is it too optimistic?

And what about Europe?

The soft power scenario

At the end of the 2020s, it must be noted that Europe has neither state nor government, but that it governs itself differently and manages to meet the expectations of its peoples. It was a long journey back. After a few troubled years, Europe returned to life. The public authorities of the EU understood late in the 2010s that they had sought to build Europe through bureaucracy and technocracy at a time when people were beginning to reject these mechanistic approaches in favor of living organizations. They also began to feel that the era was no longer centered on the paradigm of competition-negotiation but on that of optimization.

Breaking with the previous model, since the end of the 2010s, the EU has encouraged and partly funded the proliferation of European do tanks and laboratories which, freed of national and partisan points of view, seek optimal strategies for Europe, whose effectiveness has been reinforced by digital networks. The regions have gained more autonomy to carry out concrete projects corresponding to the wishes of their people.

The legal status of companies has been redefined to correspond to the transition from a financial capitalism ensuring the overall power of shareholders, to a socio-attentive economy: in France, the Pacte law has redefined the societal and environmental role of companies.

New organizations have worked on full employment, the integration of Muslim populations, the energy transition, the development of a bio-inspired industry, and reforms enabling a painless transition from a state-assisted society to a fraternal society. Europe still has no central state, but by the early 2020s, its main strategic orientations have begun to emerge from the interaction of its hybrid do tanks, which are solidly anchored in the society of people.

Part III. A great bifurcation

People rejoice in the feeling that Europe can produce the common good. Inequalities are less striking, energy transition is on track, bio-inspired techniques are flourishing, self-adjustment is working, immigrants are integrating well.

There is a sense that democracy is working better because people, collectives and businesses are participating fully in the ecosystems that involve them. They feel good in their city or region. They still feel French, Italian, or Swedish, but more and more European and proud of it. Their sense of forming a human collective with the whole world is reinforced. Coalition governments, abandoning partisan logic to focus on the pursuit of the common good, have won against populist, nation-centered governments.

Institutional DIY (Do It Yourself) is paying off. Gradually, the big choices of political orientation have moved from the national to the loco-regional and European levels. National governance bodies ensure that communication channels are in good condition and that the necessary inter-adjustments occur, while allowing the actors maximum autonomy.

In 2030, Europe is beginning to appear to the world as a human success and a bearer of peace and harmonious development. Its soft power is becoming operational. It has built a bond of trust with China, and plays a facilitating role in the tense dialogue between China and the United States, and between China and its neighbors. This example encourages others to follow.

If the European political theater can understand how a society of people can evolve, Europe will be particularly well placed on the path of humanist metamorphosis. The popular coagulation of the years 2010-2020 could announce an acceleration of the transition towards another form of democracy, unless growing challenges thwart it and open a major bifurcation offering a preponderant position to populism and its attendant authoritarianism.

Humanistic metamorphosis is seriously threatened or slowing. Can the vitality of Homo Sapiens prevail?

Chapter 12. Conclusion. Intuiting a change of era: we must take care of our humanist metamorphosis

Nothing is written in advance.

The humanist metamorphosis, which has been consistently transforming us in certain directions for almost a century, is a gift. It is readying us to meet the mortal ecological and geopolitical challenges resulting from the oversimplification of applying a rigid rationality in every walk of life.

This metamorphosis seems to offer humanity a possible jump in complexity which will open the door to a new, more adult, and more fulfilled era in our development

The metamorphosis is comprised of a set of socio-cultural processes forming a system. The system builds itself by continuous adaptation to its environment. It evolves in its own way according to persistent orientations and shaping trends, but encounters fluctuations and can bifurcate. Development can accelerate, slow down, or take breaks. Future states are not predetermined; we can try to anticipate them, but we cannot predict, plan, or order them. It is wise to let life invent its best paths without curbing it by accumulating too many barriers and precautions. Meanwhile, it is essential to maintain a vigilant surveillance and remain ready to react, either by deviating early from possibly pernicious fluctuations, or by accompanying or accelerating productive developments.

The fact that today we are better connected than before to the rational, emotional-relational and spiritual skills of our brain, and more capable of making them work together, probably increases our capacity for anticipation and conscious participation in metamorphosis.

Being more empathic and socio-perceptive than in the past, having embryonic tools of observation and analysis of socio-cultural dynamics at our disposal, if we cannot predict them, we can at least anticipate probable future trends of metamorphosis. This inchoate skill enhances our ability to participate. If we perceive the dynamics of metamorphosis well enough, we can try to work with them: to reinforce a shaping trend, to spot a perverse process early and divert it, or to catalyze a potentially life-enhancing development. By developing its socio-perceptive abilities, Homo Sapiens may become more astute in its appreciation of the future. Such interventions are necessarily approximate, tentative: one acts according to an idea for a helpful change; one observes how the system reacts; if things go in the expected direction, one persists; if not, an adjustment or other maneuver would be more appropriate.

Humanistic metamorphosis has been triggered by transformations of people's personalities and ways of life. Today, it is well advanced. Actors, through their behavior - whether individuals in their personal or professional lives, networks, collectives, business leaders, civil servants, or political leaders - contribute to or slow the metamorphosis, consciously or not. They can accompany or catalyze life-enhancing initiatives, or block them.

Conclusion

THE INTUITION OF A CHANGING ERA

As metamorphosis progresses, our society becomes more capable of wisely controlling its development and peacefully resolving its conflicts. It is better equipped to meet the ecological and geopolitical challenges of the twenty-first century.

We are doing much more than moving from a less astute to a wiser civilization. It is likely that we are leaving behind us the era of civilizations dominated by competition, hierarchy, state, appropriation of objects and territories, segmentation, competition to maximize benefits, and warlike postures. In contrast, a society of people becomes more finely meshed, less hierarchic, more self-organized, self-regulated, and driven by its own interactions. The ambition is no longer to domesticate and tame men and nature, but to help them develop. This new society of people, though infinitely more complex, is closer to that of the hunter-gatherers than to the era of pyramidal civilizations. And it seems that in the twenty-first century, several civilizations - especially Western and Chinese - are getting closer to each other, perhaps initiating the self-organization of a global socio-culture. This is the first time that a human society has brought together so many brains that are equally developed and inter-communicating. We have preserved the legacy of the West that pushed rationality further than any other civilization, accumulating unparalleled scientific and intellectual capital. But we have also developed our emotional-relational brain, now perhaps as powerful as that of hunter-gatherers. We have made contact with most human spiritualities. And the Earth's population is interconnected as it has never been, becoming a society-as-a-brain.

Humans in the twenty-first century are gaining in autonomy, vitality, and understanding of life. With instant communication between individuals, they are in a position to develop a collective intelligence, a consciousness enabling them to optimize their alliance with nature. This is a new phase of the human adventure. This optimistic intuition is not new. In the twentieth century, many Europeans and Americans had this feeling. As we said in the chapter on "the spirit of metamorphosis", Alfred Korzybski foresaw a non-Aristotelian world coming to life and the adulthood of humanity. "New Age" adepts announced a peaceful Aquarian age; Pierre Teilhard de Chardin spoke of the noosphere and the omega point. A fairly broad collective intuition foresees fundamental changes approaching, and many forecasters - including scientists, economists and neuro-scientists - describe them. Today, at the point of bifurcation, what we observe at the beginning of the 21st century justifies our being confident. But everything is possible. The metamorphosis could, as we have seen, be aborted, or be co-opted to other ends, in which case it would take a very long time to reach such a favorable period again. Are we living in "a century of the mind" centered on the humanistic metamorphosis? Will it collapse into darkness? The lights of hope will go out if we do not take care of them.

TAKING CARE OF METAMORPHOSIS

Having closed this book, perhaps you will think that our metamorphosis is a perverse myth, that we must take things in charge, go back to the authorities, the State, the struggle between classes and nations. But if you are mistaken and the metamorphosis continues, you will be out of step with your living environment and thus vulnerable. In seeking to preserve your obsolete concept of power structures, perhaps you will actually end up losing what real power you have.

HAPPYMORPHOSE

The role of each of us, networks and movements, Happymorphose

You probably have a foothold in several networks and newly formed collectivities. What are they? What does each of them bring to metamorphosis and the common good? And you yourself, what is your own contribution? Try to remember the last time you felt that your life made sense. What happened? Try to remember the last times you felt you were part of a human metamorphosis. In your personal life? In your professional life? In your civic life? What deficits in the common good seem to you the most painful in today's world? What could you personally do to help reduce them?

By reading this book you may have sharpened your empathy and socio-perception. Perhaps you feel more strongly than ever before that there are many of you - people, associations, companies, remnants of former power structures, hybrid collectives - living the adventure of humanist metamorphosis.

Hundreds of millions of people around the world are leaning in the same direction as you. You are slightly interconnected to each other and together form an incipient yet powerful movement. To help you look for other people or groups like yourself, or to offer you entry into growing ecosystems, we hope to bring you a living extension of this book: we await your reactions, comments, stories of metamorphoses through the website and blog at **www.happymorphose.com**, and email address **contact@happymorphose.com**. Each quarter, the Metamorphosis Newsletters collect and illustrate the stories of new pathways being explored. These will bring you connections, exchanges, information, and networks forming systems, that will allow you to more fully become actors in the new society of self-organized people.

At this major crossroad, the search for new pathways to the future is a question of increasing awareness, which will enable you to sense the best ways, to become an actor in the humanist metamorphosis that is self-organizing according to a fractal and nested pattern. There is no doubt that it will prove more surprising than we imagine, on our global road towards humanity's potential fulfillment.

Bibliography

Michel Aglietta et Guo Bai, *la Voie chinoise, Capitalisme et Empire*, Odile Jacob, 2012.

Jim Al-Khalili et Johnjoe McFadden, *Life on the Edge: The Coming of Age of Quantum Biology*, Bantam Press, 2014.

Lena Rachel Andersen, Tomas Björkman, *The Nordic Secret: A European History of Beauty and Freedom*, Fri Tanke Stockholm, 2017.

Alain Berthoz, *La Simplexité*, Odile Jacob, 2009.

Dominique Cardon. *La démocratie Internet: Promesses et Limites*, Paris, Seuil, 2010.

Antonio Damasio, *Self comes to Mind, constructing the conscious brain*, Panthéon, 2010.

Antonio Damasio, *Descartes' error*, 1995.

Antonio Damasio, *The strange order of things, Life, feeling and the making of cultures*, 2017.

Stanislas Dehaene, Yann Le Cun, Jacques Girardon, *La plus belle histoire de l'intelligence*, Robert Laffont, 2018.

Norbert Elias, Über den prozess der civilization, 1939.

Sigmund Freud, *Das Unbehagen in der Kultur*, 1930.

Thierry Gaudin, *L'avenir de l'esprit*, Albin Michel, 2001.

Arie de Geus, *The living company*, Harvard Business School Press, 2002.

Pierre Giorgini, *La transition fulgurante,* Bayard, 2014.

Pierre Giorgini, *La fulgurante récréation,* Bayard, 2016.

Pierre Giorgini, *Au Crépuscule des lieux,* Bayard, 2016.

Yuval Noah Harari, *Homo Deus, a brief history of Tomorrow,* Vintage, 2017.

François Jacob, *La Logique du vivant : une histoire de l'hérédité,* Paris, Gallimard, 1976.

Adam Kahane, *Power and Love,* Berrett-Koehler, 2009.

Naomi Klein, *Dire non ne suffit plus. Contre la stratégie du choc de Trump,* Paris, Actes Sud, 2017.

Alfred Korzybski, *Manhood of Humanity, The Science And Art of Human Engineering,* Institute of General Semantics, 1950.

Alfred Korzybski, *Science and Sanity, An Introduction to Non-Aristotelian Systems and General Semantics,* 1st edition, 1933.

Frédéric Laloux, *Reinventing organizations,* Nelson Parker, 2016.

James Lovelock, *Gaia, A New Look at Life On Earth,* Oxford University Press, 1979.

Jame Lovelock, *The Ages of Gaia: A Biography of Our Living Earth,* Norton, 1988.

James Lovelock, *The Revenge of Gaia, Why the Earth Is Fighting Back – And How We Can Still Save Humanity,* Penguin books, 2006.

Edgar Morin, *La Méthode,* Paris, Seuil, 2008.

Egard Morin, *On complexity,* 2008.

Edgar Morin, *Connaissance, ignorance et mystère,* Paris, Fayard, 2017.

Luiz Pessoa, *The Cognitive-Emotional Brain: From Interactions to Integration*, MIT Press, 2013.

Steven Pinker, *The Better Angels of Our Nature: Why Violence Has Declined*, New York, Penguin Random House, 2011.

Steven Pinker, *Enlightenment now: The Case for Reason, Science, Humanism and Progress*, New York, Penguin Random House, 2011.

Ilya Prigogine et Isabelle Stengers, *La Nouvelle Alliance*, Paris: Gallimard, 1979.

Ilya Prigogine and Isabelle Stengers, *Order out of chaos*, 1984.

Kate Raworth, *Doughnut Economics,* Random House Business, 2018.

Jeremy Rifkin, *The Third Industrial Revolution*, Palgrave Macmillan, 2013.

Jeremy Rifkin, *The End of Work, the decline of the global workforce and the dawn of the post-market era,* Jeremy P. Tarcher, 1995.

Jeremy Rifkin, *The Zero marginal Cost society*, Palgrave Macmillan, 2014.

Giacomo Rizzolatti et Corrado Sinigaglia, *The Mirror Neuron system,* NCBI, 2009.

Joël de Rosnay, *La symphonie du vivant, comment l'épigénétique va changer notre vie,* Paris, Les liens qui libèrent, 2018.

Peter Senge, *The Fifth Discipline,* MIT, Sloan School of Management, Cambridge, USA, 1990.

Peter Senge, *Dance of change, the challenges of sustaining momentum in learning organizations,* New-York, Double Day, 1999.

Peter Senge, *Schools that learn,* Nicholas Brealey publishing, 2000.

Peter Senge, *Presence, Human purpose and the field of the future,* with Otto Scharmer, Joseph Jaworski, Betty Sue, SoL, Cambridge, Crown Business, USA, 2008.

Peter Senge, *The necessary revolution, How individuals and organizations are working together to create a sustainable world,* Double day, 2008.

Michel Serres, *C'était mieux avant !,* Manifestes Le Pommier, 2017.

Michel Serres, *Petite poucette,* Manifestes Le Pommier, 2012.

Steven Taylor*, The Fall: The Insanity of the Ego in Human History and the Dawning of a New Era,* Iff Books, 2018.

Lily L. Tsai, *Accountability Without Democracy: Solidarity Groups and Public Goods Provision in Rural China,* Cambridge University Press, 2007.

Francisco Varela, *Autonomie et Connaissance,* Paris, Seuil, 1989.

Alain de Vulpian, *À l'écoute des gens ordinaires, comment ils transforment le monde,* Paris, Dunod, 2003.

Alain de Vulpian, *Towards the third modernity, how ordinary people are transforming the world,* Axminster, UK, 2008.

Alain de Vulpian, *Éloge de la métamorphose, en marche vers une nouvelle humanité,* grand prix de l'essai Académie Française, 2e edition, 2021.

Alain de Vulpian, *Homo Sapiens à l'heure de l'intelligence artificielle*, Eyrolles, 2019.

Frans de Waal, *The age of empathy, Nature's lessons for a kinder society*, 2009.

Acknowledgements

To all you readers working towards metamorphosis and who pass this book on.

To Patrick Degrave, Pierre Giorgini, Yves le Floc'h Soye, Patrick Lener, Sean Lafleur, Kevin Dolgin, Heidi Sparkes Guber, Anne Beaufumé, for their contribution to this updated edition.

To Sophie Juin for the graphic design of the cover page.

To Claire-Agnès Gueutin for her layout work and for publishing this book.

To Göran Carstedt, Tomas Björkman and the Ekskäret Foundation, Alexandra Mitsotaki and Irène Papaligouras, founders of the World Human Forum in Delphi and all the members of Happymorphose who are committed to the internationalization of this book, especially Gilles Poirieux and EVH, Christian Maisonneuve, and the Catholic University of Lille.

To the association SoL France which supported the development of Happymorphose.

To Richard Maxwell, the translator, and Adela Cosijn.

Facing tsunamis,

a confident and pragmatic view

of a world in metamorphosis

Your world

This is <u>your</u> story

Happymorphose

— includes people from all walks of life: business, government, associations, unions, local authorities...,
— identifies initiatives that can change the world,
— takes care of our humanity.

www.happymorphose.com

HAPPYMORPHOSE